API DEVELOPMENT FUNDAMENTALS
WITH FLASK

Master the Art of Building Scalable and Secure APIs with Flask

SIMON TELLIER

Table of Contents

between incompatible type systems (e.g., between Python objects and relational databases). SQLAlchemy is a popular ORM used with Flask.   251

6. Endpoint: A specific URL pattern in an API where the client can send a request. For example, /users could be an endpoint for retrieving user data.   251

7. CRUD: Acronym for Create, Read, Update, Delete. These are the basic operations performed on data in most APIs.   251

8. Blueprint: A way to organize your Flask application into reusable components, allowing you to break the app into smaller, manageable parts.   251

9. Middleware: Code that sits between the request and response phases of an API call. Flask supports middleware functions to handle things like authentication and logging.   251

10. CORS (Cross-Origin Resource Sharing): A security feature that allows or blocks web browsers from making requests to a domain different from the one the page was served from.   251

11. WebSocket: A protocol that provides full-duplex communication channels over a single TCP connection, allowing real-time data exchange.   251

CHAPTER 1: INTRODUCTION TO API DEVELOPMENT WITH FLASK

1.1 UNDERSTANDING API DEVELOPMENT

In today's digital landscape, APIs (Application Programming Interfaces) have become the backbone of modern web applications. They allow different software systems to communicate with each other, enabling a seamless exchange of data and functionality. Whether it's integrating with external services, connecting mobile apps to backend systems, or facilitating data sharing across platforms, APIs are at the heart of much of the technology we use daily.

API development involves creating these interfaces that allow one application to interact with another. The beauty of an API lies in its simplicity: it allows a system to send a request to another system and receive a response, typically in a standardized format like JSON or XML. This simplicity enables developers to build powerful, scalable, and interoperable systems.

When building APIs, it's important to understand the key components involved:

- **Endpoints:** The URLs where API requests are sent. Each endpoint corresponds to a specific function or resource.
- **HTTP Methods:** The standard methods used to interact with APIs. These include GET (retrieve data), POST (create data), PUT (update data), DELETE (remove data), and others.
- **Request and Response:** The core of API interactions. A request is made from a client (like a web browser or mobile app) to a server, which processes the request and sends a response back.

1

- **Status Codes:** These are returned in responses to indicate the success or failure of the request. Codes like 200 (OK), 404 (Not Found), and 500 (Internal Server Error) are commonly used to communicate the outcome.

API development focuses on defining clear, well-structured endpoints, ensuring efficient data handling, and implementing secure communication. Over time, APIs have evolved to support more complex use cases, such as REST (Representational State Transfer), which relies on standard web protocols like HTTP and emphasizes scalability and simplicity.

In this chapter, we'll introduce you to the fundamentals of API development, focusing on creating APIs using Flask, a Python web framework. Flask is lightweight, flexible, and ideal for building APIs due to its simple yet powerful architecture.

1.2 Overview of Flask and Why It's Perfect for APIs

Flask is a Python-based web framework that has gained immense popularity for building web applications and APIs. Created by Armin Ronacher in 2010, Flask follows a minimalist approach, meaning it doesn't come with a lot of built-in tools or structure like some other frameworks (such as Django). Instead, Flask gives developers the freedom to choose their tools and structure their application however they like.

This lightweight nature makes Flask a fantastic choice for developers looking to create custom APIs. Whether you're building a small, single-function API or a complex, multi-endpoint system, Flask allows you to get up and running quickly without unnecessary overhead.

Here are some of the key reasons why Flask is perfect for API development:

- **Minimalism and Flexibility:** Flask doesn't impose any constraints on how you structure your application. This makes it a great choice for developers who want full control over their code. You can decide which libraries to integrate and how to organize your project based on your specific needs.

- **Simplicity:** Flask's core API is easy to understand and use. With just a few lines of code, you can create a fully functional API endpoint. This simplicity makes Flask an excellent choice for both beginners and seasoned developers.

- **Extensibility:** While Flask is minimal by design, it is highly extensible. Flask provides a number of plugins and extensions that can be easily added to your project. Whether it's adding support for database integration, user authentication, or data validation, Flask has an extension for almost every need.

- **Large Community and Documentation:** Flask benefits from a strong, active community of developers, which means you can find help and resources easily. Flask's official documentation is comprehensive and well-maintained, making it easy to get started and find solutions to common problems.

- **Ideal for RESTful APIs:** Flask is perfectly suited for creating RESTful APIs, thanks to its support for routing and handling HTTP requests. With Flask, you can easily map URLs to functions, making it simple to implement the CRUD (Create, Read, Update, Delete) operations that are foundational to most APIs.

- **Support for Testing and Debugging:** Flask comes with a built-in development server and tools that make it easy to test and debug your API. The lightweight nature of Flask means that it's quick to run, allowing you to iterate rapidly and fix bugs efficiently.

- **Scalability:** While Flask is a minimal framework, it can be used to build scalable APIs. By combining Flask with other tools and technologies (like database systems, caching, or load balancers), you can scale your Flask application to handle high traffic loads.

Flask is particularly favored by developers who value flexibility and control over their project. It's a perfect choice for anyone looking to create a straightforward API without the complexity of a heavyweight framework. For beginners, Flask offers a simple entry point into the world of web development, while more experienced developers can leverage Flask's flexibility to create sophisticated and powerful APIs.

In this book, we'll explore how to leverage Flask's simplicity, flexibility, and extensibility to create secure, scalable, and efficient APIs.

1.3 Setting Up the Development Environment

Before diving into creating APIs with Flask, we need to set up the development environment. This section will guide you through installing the necessary tools and ensuring that you're ready to start building APIs.

Step 1: Install Python

Flask is a Python web framework, so the first step is to make sure that Python is installed on your system. To check if Python is already installed, open a terminal or command prompt and type:

css

Copy

```
python --version
```

If Python is installed, you'll see the version number. If not, you'll need to install it. You can download Python from the official website: https://www.python.org/downloads/.

During installation, make sure to check the box that says "Add Python to PATH." This will allow you to run Python commands from any directory on your system.

Step 2: Set Up a Virtual Environment

When working on Python projects, it's a best practice to use a virtual environment. A virtual environment allows you to create an isolated space for your project's dependencies, ensuring that your project doesn't interfere with other Python projects on your system.

To create a virtual environment, follow these steps:

Install virtualenv:

Open a terminal and run the following command to install the virtualenv package:

Copy

```
pip install virtualenv
```

1. **Create a virtual environment:**

   Navigate to the directory where you want to store your project, and run:

   Copy

   ```
   virtualenv venv
   ```

2. **Activate the virtual environment:**

   On Windows:

   Copy

   ```
   .\venv\Scripts\activate
   ```

On macOS/Linux:

bash

Copy

```
source venv/bin/activate
```

3. After activation, your terminal prompt should change to show the name of the virtual environment (e.g., (venv)).

Step 3: Install Flask

Now that you have your virtual environment set up, the next step is to install Flask. With the virtual environment activated, run the following command:

Copy

```
pip install Flask
```

This will install the latest version of Flask and its dependencies.

Step 4: Verify Installation

To ensure Flask was installed correctly, create a simple Python file (e.g., app.py) in your project directory. Open the file and add the following code:

python
Copy

```
from flask import Flask

app = Flask(__name__)

@app.route('/')
def hello():
    return 'Hello, Flask!'

if __name__ == '__main__':
    app.run(debug=True)
```

This is a very basic Flask application that returns "Hello, Flask!" when you visit the root URL. To run the application, open your terminal, navigate to your project directory, and run:

Copy

```
python app.py
```

You should see output indicating that the Flask server is running. Open a web browser and navigate to http://127.0.0.1:5000/. You should see the message "Hello, Flask!" displayed in your browser.

Step 5: Set Up Code Editor

While not strictly necessary, using a code editor with good support for Python can make the development process easier. Some popular editors for Python development include:

- **Visual Studio Code (VSCode):** A lightweight, open-source editor with great Python support through extensions.
- **PyCharm:** A powerful, feature-rich IDE specifically designed for Python development.
- **Sublime Text:** A fast and customizable text editor with Python syntax highlighting.

Choose the editor you're most comfortable with, and make sure to install any relevant Python extensions or plugins to enhance your development workflow.

Step 6: Version Control with Git (Optional but Recommended)

As your projects grow, it's a good idea to use version control to track changes and collaborate with others. Git is the most popular version control system, and GitHub is a widely-used platform for hosting code.

To set up Git for your project, run the following commands in your project directory:

csharp

Copy

```
git init
```

```
git add .
git commit -m "Initial commit"
```

This will initialize a Git repository, add your project files, and commit them with a message.

1.4 Your First Flask API: A Step-by-Step Guide

Now that your development environment is set up and Flask is installed, it's time to create your very first API. We'll start with something simple: a basic "Hello, World!" API. From there, we will gradually introduce you to more advanced concepts and features.

Step 1: Create a Simple Flask Application

Open your code editor and create a new file, app.py, in your project directory. The first step is to import Flask and create an instance of the Flask class. This instance will represent your application.

```python
Copy
from flask import Flask

app = Flask(__name__)
```

Here, we're importing Flask and initializing the application. The __name__ argument passed to Flask is a special Python variable that tells Flask where to look for the application. It helps Flask know where to search for resources like templates and static files.

8

Step 2: Define an API Endpoint

Next, we'll define a simple route. A route is a URL pattern that Flask will associate with a specific function in your application. When a user visits the URL corresponding to this route, Flask will execute the associated function and return a response.

Let's define a basic route that returns a "Hello, World!" message:

python

Copy

```python
@app.route('/')
def hello_world():
    return 'Hello, World!'
```

In this code:

- @app.route('/') is a decorator that maps the URL path '/' (the root URL) to the hello_world function.
- The hello_world function returns a simple string, "Hello, World!" when the endpoint is hit.

Step 3: Run the Flask Application

Now, let's run the Flask application. Below the route definition, add the following code to run the app in development mode:

python

Copy

```python
if __name__ == '__main__':
    app.run(debug=True)
```

Here, app.run(debug=True) starts the Flask development server, which will automatically reload the app whenever you make changes to the code. The debug=True option enables debugging mode, which provides detailed error messages and helpful information if something goes wrong.

To run the application, open your terminal, navigate to your project directory, and run the following command:

Copy

```
python app.py
```

After running this command, you should see output like this:

csharp

Copy

```
* Running on http://127.0.0.1:5000/ (Press CTRL+C to quit)
```

Now, open your web browser and go to http://127.0.0.1:5000/. You should see the message "Hello, World!" displayed in your browser.

Step 4: Testing the API

Now that your Flask API is running, let's test it using curl or a tool like Postman. Open a new terminal window and run the following command:

arduino

Copy

```
curl http://127.0.0.1:5000/
```

You should see the same "Hello, World!" message as the response. If you prefer a more graphical interface for testing, Postman is a great tool for sending HTTP requests to your

10

API. With Postman, you can send requests like GET, POST, PUT, and DELETE, and view the responses.

Step 5: Adding More Routes

Now that you've created your first API route, it's time to expand the application. Let's add another endpoint that returns a greeting with a name:

python

Copy

```python
@app.route('/greet/<name>')
def greet(name):
    return f'Hello, {name}!'
```

Here, we've added a dynamic part to the URL using Flask's route parameter <name>. When you visit a URL like /greet/John, Flask will pass "John" as the argument to the greet function. The function will then return a greeting using that name.

To test this, restart your Flask server, and visit http://127.0.0.1:5000/greet/John in your browser. You should see "Hello, John!" displayed.

1.5 Key Flask Concepts: Routes, Views, and Request Handling

Now that you've created your first Flask API, it's important to understand some of the key concepts that will help you build more sophisticated APIs. In this section, we'll dive deeper into routes, views, and request handling.

Routes

A route in Flask is simply a URL pattern that is associated with a function. This function is called a view, and it returns a response when the route is accessed.

11

In Flask, you define routes using decorators. For example:

python

Copy

```python
@app.route('/')
def home():
    return 'Welcome to the homepage!'
```

When a user visits the root URL /, Flask will call the home function and return the string "Welcome to the homepage!"

Routes can include dynamic parts, such as parameters, that allow you to create flexible APIs. For example:

python

Copy

```python
@app.route('/greet/<name>')
def greet(name):
    return f'Hello, {name}!'
```

Here, <name> is a dynamic route parameter, which Flask captures and passes to the view function as a variable.

Views

A view in Flask is simply a function that handles a request and returns a response. The response could be a string, a file, or even a JSON object, depending on the needs of your API.

You can create views for different HTTP methods. For example:

python

Copy

```python
@app.route('/data', methods=['POST'])
def create_data():
    return 'Data created', 201
```

In this example, the create_data function is only called when the client sends a POST request to /data. Similarly, you can define views for GET, PUT, and DELETE requests to handle various actions.

Request Handling

Flask provides a simple and intuitive way to handle HTTP requests. When a client sends a request to an endpoint, Flask provides an object called request that you can use to access details about the request.

For example, to access query parameters sent with a GET request:

python

Copy

```python
from flask import request

@app.route('/search')
def search():
    query = request.args.get('q')
    return f'Search results for {query}'
```

Here, we use request.args.get('q') to get the value of the query parameter q sent with the request, such as ?q=python.

Flask also makes it easy to handle POST data, which is often used when submitting forms or sending JSON data:

python
Copy

```python
@app.route('/submit', methods=['POST'])
def submit():
    data = request.form['data']
    return f'You submitted: {data}'
```

In this case, the request.form object is used to access form data sent with a POST request.

Response Handling

In Flask, the view function must return a response. By default, Flask returns a string as a response, but you can also return other types of responses. For example, you can return JSON data:

python
Copy

```python
from flask import jsonify

@app.route('/data')
def get_data():
    data = {'name': 'Flask', 'type': 'Web Framework'}
    return jsonify(data)
```

In this case, jsonify is a helper function that converts Python dictionaries or lists into JSON format, which is a common data format used in APIs.

You can also set custom HTTP status codes by returning a tuple:

python
Copy
```
return 'Created', 201
```

In this case, 201 is the HTTP status code for "Created," indicating that the resource was successfully created.

1.6 Summary & What's Next

In this chapter, you learned the fundamentals of API development with Flask. You've created your first API, defined routes, and explored how to handle HTTP requests and responses. Here's a quick recap of what we've covered:

- **API Development Basics:** We discussed the importance of APIs and how they enable communication between different software systems.
- **Overview of Flask:** We introduced Flask as a lightweight, flexible framework for building APIs and web applications.
- **Setting Up the Development Environment:** You set up Python, created a virtual environment, and installed Flask, preparing your system for development.
- **Creating Your First Flask API:** You built a simple "Hello, World!" API and learned how to define routes and handle requests.
- **Key Flask Concepts:** You explored important Flask concepts, including routes, views, request handling, and response handling.

In the next chapter, we'll dive deeper into the core principles of API design. We'll explore RESTful API design, which is essential for building APIs that are easy to use, scalable, and maintainable. You'll also learn best practices for structuring your API and ensuring it's future-proof.

By now, you should feel comfortable creating simple APIs with Flask. As we continue this journey, we'll build on these foundational concepts and introduce more advanced topics, including database integration, security, and optimization, to help you build powerful, production-ready APIs.

Chapter 2: Fundamental Principles of API Design

2.1 What Makes a Great API?

APIs are the connectors that allow applications to communicate with one another. Whether you are creating a small internal service or a public API that will be used by thousands of developers, the principles of designing a great API remain largely the same. A well-designed API can be a game-changer, offering not only functionality but also an intuitive, seamless user experience. But what exactly makes an API "great"? Let's break it down.

1. Simplicity

The best APIs are often the simplest. A great API should have a clear and easy-to-understand interface, even for new users. When a developer first encounters your API, it should be immediately clear how to interact with it. This means:

- **Clear Naming Conventions:** Use clear and descriptive names for your endpoints, methods, and parameters. For example, an endpoint that retrieves user data should be named something like /users, and actions like creating, updating, or deleting users should use intuitive HTTP methods like POST, PUT, and DELETE.
- **Logical Structure:** Group related functionality together and ensure that your API has a logical and predictable structure. Users should be able to guess where to find an endpoint based on its name.

2. Consistency

Consistency is key to making your API easy to understand and use. Every aspect of your API should follow consistent patterns. For instance:

- **Naming Consistency:** Stick to one naming convention for endpoints. If you choose camelCase (like /getUserData), stick with it throughout your API.
- **Method Consistency:** Always use the correct HTTP method for each action. For example, don't use POST for retrieving data; GET should be used for that purpose. Similarly, avoid using GET for actions that modify server-side data.

3. Predictability

A great API should behave in predictable ways. When developers interact with your API, they should be able to anticipate the results based on their actions. This includes:

- **HTTP Status Codes:** Use standard HTTP status codes that accurately describe the outcome of an API request. For example, a successful request should return a 200 OK status code, and a failed request due to incorrect input should return a 400 Bad Request.
- **Response Formats:** Return responses in a consistent format. JSON is the most common format for APIs today because it is easy to parse and use. When developers know what format to expect, they can quickly build tools to interact with your API.

4. Documentation

Good documentation is often the difference between a successful and unsuccessful API. A great API comes with clear, comprehensive, and up-to-date documentation that explains how to use the API, what each endpoint does, and what parameters are required. The documentation should include:

- **Examples:** Code snippets that show how to make requests to the API, both for simple cases and for more complex ones.
- **Error Handling:** Explain the common errors users might encounter and how to fix them.

- **Authentication and Authorization:** If your API requires authentication, provide detailed steps on how to set it up.

5. Flexibility

A great API is flexible enough to support future use cases and changes. Consider the following:

- **Versioning:** Always plan for versioning your API. As new features are added or existing ones are changed, versioning ensures that existing users aren't disrupted. A typical approach is to include the version number in the URL, such as /v1/users.
- **Extensibility:** The API should be easily extendable. Developers should be able to add new features to their own application without having to worry about breaking existing functionality in your API.

6. Performance

Performance matters, especially when your API will be used by a large number of users. A great API should be optimized for fast responses and minimal resource usage. Some tips for improving performance:

- **Caching:** Use caching mechanisms to avoid hitting the server for repeated requests. For example, if data doesn't change frequently, cache it and return the cached version on subsequent requests.
- **Rate Limiting:** Implement rate limiting to protect your API from being overwhelmed by too many requests in a short amount of time.

7. Security

Security is another critical aspect of a great API. Exposing sensitive data or giving attackers an easy way to exploit vulnerabilities is a recipe for disaster. Some key points for securing an API:

- **Authentication:** Use strong authentication methods, such as OAuth or JWT (JSON Web Tokens), to ensure that only authorized users can access your API.
- **Encryption:** Use HTTPS (TLS/SSL) to encrypt data in transit and protect it from eavesdropping.
- **Input Validation:** Always validate user input to prevent malicious data from being processed.

8. Error Handling

Clear error messages and handling are essential for making your API user-friendly. A great API provides detailed error messages that help developers quickly identify what went wrong and how to fix it. For example:

- **400 Bad Request:** When the user submits invalid data.
- **404 Not Found:** When the requested resource doesn't exist.
- **500 Internal Server Error:** For server-side issues that need to be addressed.

2.2 Introduction to RESTful API Design

REST (Representational State Transfer) is an architectural style for building web services that has become the gold standard for designing APIs. A RESTful API is one that adheres to the principles of REST, providing an efficient, scalable, and stateless way to communicate between clients and servers. Understanding REST is crucial for building APIs that are both powerful and easy to use.

1. The Basics of REST

RESTful APIs are based on a set of well-defined principles that make them flexible, scalable, and easy to integrate with. Here are the key principles of RESTful design:

- **Statelessness:** Each request from a client to the server must contain all the information needed to understand and process the request. The server does not store any session data between requests. Each request is treated independently, which allows for better scalability and simpler error handling.
- **Client-Server Architecture:** REST follows a client-server model, where the client and the server are separate entities. The client sends requests to the server, and the server processes those requests and returns the appropriate response.
- **Uniform Interface:** REST APIs have a uniform interface, meaning that all interactions between the client and the server happen via a set of standard conventions. This simplifies the system and makes it easier to understand and interact with.

2. RESTful API Methods

In RESTful API design, HTTP methods are used to perform operations on resources. Each resource (such as a user, product, or blog post) can be accessed using standard HTTP methods. These methods are:

- **GET:** Retrieves data from the server. This is used for reading resources. Example: GET /users retrieves a list of users.
- **POST:** Creates a new resource on the server. Example: POST /users creates a new user.
- **PUT:** Updates an existing resource. Example: PUT /users/1 updates the user with ID 1.
- **DELETE:** Deletes a resource from the server. Example: DELETE /users/1 deletes the user with ID 1.

These methods align perfectly with the CRUD (Create, Read, Update, Delete) operations, which are essential for any API dealing with data.

3. Resources and Endpoints

In REST, resources are the main objects that the API interacts with. Each resource should have a unique URL, and these URLs should reflect the structure of the data being handled. For example:

- **/users:** Represents a collection of user resources.
- **/users/1:** Represents a specific user with the ID of 1.
- **/posts:** Represents a collection of blog post resources.
- **/posts/5:** Represents a specific blog post with ID 5.

The use of clear, descriptive URLs ensures that your API is intuitive and easy to use.

4. JSON as the Data Format

REST APIs typically use JSON (JavaScript Object Notation) as the format for sending and receiving data. JSON is lightweight, easy to read, and widely supported across programming languages. For example, a response from a REST API might look like this:

json
Copy

```json
{
  "id": 1,
  "name": "John Doe",
  "email": "john.doe@example.com"
}
```

This JSON object represents a user, with fields for the user's ID, name, and email. JSON is flexible and can represent complex data structures, making it ideal for web services.

5. HTTP Status Codes

In REST, status codes are used to indicate the success or failure of a request. These codes are part of the HTTP response and provide valuable information about the outcome of the request. Some common status codes are:

- **200 OK:** The request was successful, and the response contains the requested data.
- **201 Created:** The request was successful, and a new resource was created.
- **400 Bad Request:** The request was invalid, often due to missing or incorrect data.
- **404 Not Found:** The requested resource does not exist.
- **500 Internal Server Error:** An error occurred on the server side.

Properly using status codes helps the client understand the result of their request and handle it accordingly.

6. Stateless Communication

In RESTful design, each API request must be independent. This is known as stateless communication. The server does not store any information about the client's previous requests. Every request from the client must include all necessary information (such as authentication tokens, parameters, etc.) to complete the request.

Statelessness helps improve scalability and simplifies the server-side implementation. It allows the server to process each request without needing to keep track of previous interactions.

2.3 Key API Design Principles

When it comes to API design, adhering to a set of key principles ensures that your API is user-friendly, maintainable, and effective. These principles are essential for creating APIs that developers enjoy using, while also making them scalable and robust enough to meet the needs of complex applications. Below are some of the most important API design principles you should follow:

1. Consistency

Consistency in your API design means that it should behave predictably across different endpoints. When developers use your API, they should be able to anticipate how different endpoints will work, based on the naming conventions and actions they perform. Consistency reduces the cognitive load on developers and makes it easier for them to integrate your API into their projects.

Some ways to ensure consistency include:

- **Naming conventions:** Use consistent naming patterns for your endpoints. For example, if you use plural nouns for resource names (e.g., /users, /posts), stick to that convention across the entire API.
- **HTTP methods:** Ensure that you always use the correct HTTP methods for their intended purposes. For example, use GET for fetching data, POST for creating data, PUT for updating data, and DELETE for removing data.

2. Simplicity

Simplicity is one of the cornerstones of great API design. A simple API reduces the learning curve for new developers and makes it easier to maintain. Keep the number of required parameters to a minimum and avoid unnecessary complexity in the API's structure.

- **Minimal required parameters:** For any given endpoint, only ask for parameters that are absolutely necessary. If an endpoint requires user authentication, don't make it more complex than it needs to be.
- **Clear documentation:** Make sure that your API's documentation is straightforward, focusing on how to get started with minimal effort. Include well-documented examples and keep things easy to follow.

3. Discoverability

Your API should be easy to explore. A developer should be able to understand what the API does, what resources it handles, and how to interact with it just by reading the documentation or browsing the endpoints. Some ways to improve discoverability include:

- **Clear, descriptive endpoints:** Make sure each endpoint name clearly reflects its function. For example, /users should retrieve users, and /users/{id} should return the details of a specific user.
- **Interactive documentation:** Consider using tools like Swagger or OpenAPI to create interactive documentation that allows users to try out API calls directly in the documentation. This makes it easier for developers to experiment with your API before they start integrating it into their applications.

4. Flexibility

A flexible API allows developers to use it in a wide variety of scenarios. APIs should be adaptable to changing requirements and should offer enough customization options to fit different use cases. Flexibility also refers to ensuring that your API can evolve without breaking existing functionality for developers who are already using it.

- **Optional parameters:** Allow users to pass optional parameters for filtering, sorting, or paginating responses. For example, /users?limit=10&sort=asc could allow a user to limit the results and sort them in ascending order.

- **Extensibility:** Ensure that your API is easy to extend in the future. Keep the core design flexible and modular, so that adding new features doesn't require a major overhaul of the entire API.

5. Error Handling and Feedback

Clear, informative error messages are vital for a good user experience. When something goes wrong, the API should provide enough information for the user to understand what happened and how they can fix it. Use HTTP status codes to convey the general outcome of the request and include meaningful error messages in the response body.

- **HTTP status codes:** Standardize the use of HTTP status codes, such as 200 OK, 400 Bad Request, 404 Not Found, and 500 Internal Server Error.
- **Descriptive error messages:** For non-successful requests, provide detailed error messages in the response body, which should include information about why the request failed and how the user can fix it.

6. Security

Security should always be a priority in API design. Make sure that only authorized users can access sensitive data and that communication between the client and the server is protected. A great API employs industry-standard methods for authentication, authorization, and data protection.

- **Authentication:** Use authentication methods like OAuth 2.0, API keys, or JSON Web Tokens (JWT) to ensure only authorized users can access your API.
- **Encryption:** Use HTTPS for encrypted communication between the client and the server. This prevents sensitive data from being intercepted during transmission.

7. Efficiency

Efficiency is important for improving performance and user experience. An efficient API minimizes the amount of data transferred, reduces server load, and increases response times.

- **Pagination:** When dealing with large datasets, use pagination to return results in smaller chunks. For example, /users?page=1&limit=20 could return 20 users at a time.
- **Compression:** Support response compression (e.g., gzip) to reduce the size of the data being sent over the network, improving the API's speed.

By adhering to these key principles, you can build APIs that are not only functional but also easy to use, secure, and maintain. Consistency, simplicity, and flexibility are at the heart of what makes a great API.

2.4 API Versioning and Structuring

As your API grows and evolves, there will come a time when you need to make changes that could potentially break backward compatibility. Whether it's adding new features, modifying existing behavior, or updating the data model, maintaining backward compatibility with existing users is crucial. API versioning is the practice of managing and handling changes in your API over time, so that users can continue to rely on older versions of your API without disruption.

1. Why Version Your API?

Versioning your API allows you to make changes without affecting existing clients. It enables you to evolve your API over time while maintaining the stability of previous versions. Some of the reasons to version an API include:

- **Breaking Changes:** If your API changes in a way that could break the functionality for existing clients (e.g., changing the structure of a response or removing an endpoint), versioning ensures that users of the older version are not affected.
- **New Features:** When adding new features to your API, versioning lets you release them in a new version without impacting clients using the old version.

2. Common API Versioning Strategies

There are several approaches to API versioning, each with its pros and cons. The most common strategies include:

URL Path Versioning (Most Common): The version is included as part of the URL path. This is the most widely used method because it's easy to implement and provides clear versioning for the API.

Example:

bash

Copy

```
/v1/users

/v2/users
```

- **Query Parameter Versioning:** The version is included as a query parameter in the URL. This method is simple and doesn't require changes to the URL path. However, it can be less obvious which version the API is using.
  Example:
  bash
  Copy
  ```
  /users?version=1
  ```

- **Header Versioning:** The version is specified in the request headers. This is a less common approach but can be useful when you want to keep URLs clean and hide the version from the client.

  Example:

  bash

  Copy

  Accept: application/vnd.myapi.v1+json

- **Content-Type Versioning:** Similar to header versioning, this approach specifies the version in the Content-Type or Accept header, using media type parameters.

  Example:

  css

  Copy

  Content-Type: application/json; version=1.0

3. Best Practices for API Versioning

- **Start with Versioning Early:** Even if your API is in its early stages, it's a good practice to add versioning from the start. This ensures that you won't have to refactor your API later when changes are needed.
- **Keep Versioning Simple:** Stick to simple, predictable versioning schemes. Avoid complex versioning strategies that could confuse users.
- **Deprecate Old Versions Gracefully:** When you release a new version, give users plenty of time to transition to the latest version. Provide deprecation warnings and consider offering support for older versions for a reasonable amount of time.

2.5 Designing Your API for Scalability

As your application grows and your API usage increases, scalability becomes a critical concern. Designing your API with scalability in mind ensures that it can handle increased traffic and large datasets without sacrificing performance. Below are key strategies for designing scalable APIs.

1. Statelessness

One of the key principles of REST is statelessness, which means that each API request is independent of previous requests. Stateless APIs are easier to scale because the server does not need to remember previous requests. Every request includes all the information necessary to process it, which reduces the load on the server.

2. Load Balancing

As your API becomes more popular, it's important to distribute traffic across multiple servers to prevent any single server from becoming overwhelmed. Load balancing ensures that requests are evenly distributed to different servers, improving the performance and reliability of your API.

3. Caching

Caching can significantly reduce the load on your API and speed up response times by storing frequently requested data temporarily. You can use caching techniques like in-memory caching (e.g., Redis) to reduce the need to query the database or perform expensive computations for every request.

4. Pagination

When working with large datasets, returning all the data at once can be inefficient and cause performance issues. Pagination allows you to break large datasets into smaller chunks, delivering only the data that's necessary for the current request. For example, returning a list of 10 users per page helps manage server load and reduces response time.

5. Asynchronous Processing

For certain API operations (such as sending email notifications, processing large datasets, or interacting with slow external services), using asynchronous processing can improve performance. With asynchronous tasks, your API can handle multiple requests concurrently, freeing up resources and ensuring a responsive user experience.

6. Database Optimization

As your API scales, database performance can become a bottleneck. Optimize your database by:

- **Indexing:** Index the fields that are frequently queried to speed up lookups.
- **Sharding:** Split large databases into smaller, more manageable parts (shards) that can be distributed across multiple servers.

7. Rate Limiting

To prevent abuse and ensure fair usage of your API, implement rate limiting. Rate limiting restricts the number of requests a user can make in a specific time period. This protects your servers from being overwhelmed by too many requests and ensures that all users have a fair experience.

By implementing these scalability techniques, you can ensure that your API can handle a growing number of users and requests without compromising performance.

2.6 Best Practices for API Documentation

API documentation is one of the most important aspects of designing a user-friendly and effective API. Clear, comprehensive documentation not only helps developers understand how to use your API but also ensures that they can integrate it quickly and efficiently. Great documentation serves as both a reference guide and a learning tool for developers, offering examples, detailed explanations, and error handling insights.

Here are some best practices to follow when creating API documentation that will make your API more approachable and easier to use:

1. Start with an Overview

The first section of your API documentation should provide a high-level overview of what your API does and the problems it solves. This is especially helpful for new users who may be evaluating your API for the first time. The overview should include:

- **Purpose of the API:** What is the goal of the API? What kind of data or functionality does it provide?
- **Core Features:** Highlight the key features and capabilities of the API. For example, if it's a weather API, mention what types of weather data can be retrieved (temperature, humidity, forecast, etc.).
- **Authentication Methods:** Provide a brief explanation of how to authenticate with the API (e.g., API key, OAuth).

2. Provide Clear and Descriptive Endpoint Information

For each API endpoint, the documentation should clearly describe:

- **The Endpoint URL:** Provide the full URL for each endpoint, including any path parameters. For example, /users/{id} where {id} is a dynamic parameter representing the user's unique identifier.

- **Supported HTTP Methods:** Specify which HTTP methods (GET, POST, PUT, DELETE) can be used with the endpoint.
- **Description of the Endpoint:** Explain what the endpoint does and what type of data it processes or returns.
- **Parameters:** List and explain all parameters required or optional for the request. For example, a GET /users endpoint might have optional query parameters like ?page=1&limit=10.
- **Request and Response Format:** Describe the structure of the request body (if applicable) and the format of the response. For example, if the endpoint returns JSON, provide a sample response.
- **Examples:** Include sample requests and responses to demonstrate how the endpoint is used. This can help developers understand exactly what to expect when interacting with your API.
- **Error Codes:** Include possible error codes and explanations of when and why they might occur, such as 404 Not Found or 400 Bad Request.

3. Include Authentication and Authorization Details

If your API requires authentication (and most APIs do), your documentation should explain how users can authenticate. This section should cover:

- **Types of Authentication:** Describe whether your API uses API keys, OAuth tokens, or another method for authentication.
- **Obtaining Credentials:** Explain how users can obtain authentication credentials (e.g., how to generate an API key).
- **Authorization Flow:** If applicable, explain how users can manage their permissions or roles (e.g., read-only access, admin access).

4. Use Interactive Tools and Swagger/OpenAPI

Interactive documentation tools, such as Swagger or OpenAPI, allow developers to try out the API directly from the documentation. This is one of the best ways to engage users and give them a hands-on experience with your API. These tools automatically generate API documentation and can often include interactive features like:

- **Making API Requests:** Allow users to send requests directly from the documentation and view responses in real-time.
- **Request/Response Examples:** Show what a request looks like, and display the expected response based on that request.
- **Dynamic Parameter Inputs:** Allow users to experiment with different parameter values and see how the API responds.

5. Include Error Handling Information

Error handling is a key part of good API documentation. Developers need to know how to handle errors when they occur. Your documentation should include:

- **Common Error Codes:** Include explanations for common error codes and what they mean (e.g., 400 Bad Request, 401 Unauthorized, 500 Internal Server Error).
- **Error Responses:** Provide sample error responses, including the error message and any additional information that will help developers fix the issue.
- **Guidance on Troubleshooting:** Offer suggestions for what developers should check if they encounter an error, such as verifying authentication credentials or ensuring required parameters are included in the request.

6. Organize Documentation in a Logical Structure

A well-structured document is easy to navigate, even when it contains a lot of information. The following sections should be included to create a clear and logical flow:

- **Introduction/Overview:** The first section should summarize what the API does and provide an overview of key concepts.
- **Getting Started:** This section should provide step-by-step instructions on how to set up and authenticate with the API.

- **Endpoints:** List each endpoint, its parameters, request and response examples, and potential error codes.
- **Authentication:** If the API requires authentication, dedicate a section to explain the process.
- **Examples and Use Cases:** Provide example use cases to help developers understand common scenarios.
- **Error Handling and Troubleshooting:** Describe common errors, their causes, and how to resolve them.
- **Versioning and Changelog:** Include a section detailing any changes made to the API, including new features, bug fixes, or deprecated endpoints.

7. Keep Documentation Up-to-Date

As your API evolves, your documentation must evolve with it. Regularly update the documentation to reflect any changes to the API, including:

- **New Features or Endpoints:** Add documentation for new endpoints or changes to existing ones.
- **Deprecations:** Remove or mark deprecated endpoints and explain what users should do instead.
- **Bug Fixes or Updates:** Include information about bug fixes or performance improvements, and how they affect the API.

8. Provide Code Snippets and SDKs

Provide code samples in common programming languages (such as Python, JavaScript, Java, or Ruby) to help developers integrate your API into their applications. Additionally, offering SDKs (Software Development Kits) in popular languages can make it even easier for developers to get started.

9. Version Control for Documentation

Just as you version your API, it's important to version your documentation as well. This helps users know which version of the API the documentation is referring to, especially when the API evolves over time. Consider maintaining different sections of documentation for each major version of your API.

2.7 Summary & What's Next

In this chapter, we've covered the essential principles of API design that will guide you in creating APIs that are not only functional but also user-friendly, scalable, and secure. Here's a quick recap of the key points:

- **What Makes a Great API:** A great API is simple, consistent, predictable, and secure. It should be flexible enough to handle future changes without breaking existing clients.
- **RESTful API Design:** We explored the basics of REST and how it helps structure your API with clear endpoints, appropriate HTTP methods, and consistent response formats.
- **Key API Design Principles:** We discussed the importance of consistency, simplicity, discoverability, and flexibility, as well as the need for comprehensive error handling and feedback.
- **API Versioning and Structuring:** Versioning is crucial for managing API evolution while maintaining compatibility with existing clients. We covered the most common versioning strategies, such as URL path versioning and query parameter versioning.
- **Designing for Scalability:** Designing APIs to handle growth is key. We discussed techniques like stateless communication, load balancing, caching, and rate limiting to ensure your API can scale effectively.

- **Best Practices for API Documentation:** Clear, comprehensive documentation is vital for an API's success. We highlighted the need for an overview, endpoint details, examples, error handling, and how to keep documentation up to date.

As you move forward, the next step is to dive deeper into implementing these principles in real-world applications. In the following chapters, we'll explore how to implement these design patterns within Flask, looking at building secure, scalable APIs that are ready for production.

In the next chapter, we'll tackle more advanced topics, such as how to integrate databases, handle authentication and authorization, and implement robust error handling, to ensure your APIs meet the highest standards of reliability and security.

Chapter 3: Flask Basics for API Development

3.1 Flask Architecture: Understanding the Core Components

Flask is a minimalistic web framework, meaning it provides the basic tools needed to build web applications and APIs without imposing too much structure. Despite its simplicity, Flask is powerful, and understanding its core components will help you build robust APIs with it.

The Flask architecture is built around a few key components that come together to handle incoming requests, process them, and send back appropriate responses. Here's a breakdown of the primary components:

1. Flask Application Instance (Flask)

At the heart of every Flask application is the Flask class, which is used to create an application instance. This instance represents the web application and provides methods for routing, error handling, configuration, and more.

```python
Copy
from flask import Flask

app = Flask(__name__)
```

In this example, the Flask object app is the main point of interaction with the application. The __name__ argument tells Flask how to find resources like templates and static files. This instance manages routing, request handling, and configuration, and serves as the foundation of the Flask application.

38

2. Routes and Views

Flask uses the concept of **routes** to link specific URLs to functions (called **views**) that handle the request. Routes determine which code should be executed when a user accesses a specific URL. Views are the functions that respond to HTTP requests made to these routes.

For example, here's how a simple route is defined:

python

Copy

```
@app.route('/')
def home():
    return 'Welcome to the Flask API!'
```

In this example:

- The @app.route('/') decorator links the / URL path to the home() function.
- The home() function returns the string "Welcome to the Flask API!" when accessed.

You can also define dynamic routes with placeholders in the URL path, allowing you to capture variables from the URL and pass them to the view function:

python

Copy

```
@app.route('/user/<username>')
def show_user(username):
    return f'User: {username}'
```

39

Here, the <username> part is a dynamic route parameter. When a user accesses /user/john, Flask will call the show_user() function, passing the value "john" to the username parameter.

3. Request and Response Cycle

Flask handles HTTP requests and generates responses as part of its core functionality. When a user sends an HTTP request to the server, Flask processes the request and returns an appropriate response.

The **request** is the data sent from the client (e.g., a browser or mobile app) to the server, and the **response** is the data sent back to the client. Flask provides tools for both handling the incoming request and constructing the outgoing response.

4. Middleware (Wsgi)

Flask is built on top of WSGI (Web Server Gateway Interface), which is a specification for how web servers communicate with web applications in Python. WSGI acts as the middleware layer between the Flask app and the web server (like Gunicorn, Nginx, or Apache).

This architecture allows Flask to handle HTTP requests and responses in a standardized way, making it scalable and compatible with a variety of web servers.

5. Templates and Static Files

Although not essential for building APIs, Flask also provides support for templates (HTML files) and static files (CSS, JavaScript, images). In Flask-based web applications, templates are typically used to dynamically generate HTML pages, while static files are used for non-dynamic content like images or styles.

For API development, you may not interact with these directly, but understanding their purpose is helpful if you need to extend your Flask application beyond an API.

3.2 Working with Flask's Request and Response Objects

Flask makes handling requests and generating responses easy through its built-in **request** and **response** objects. These objects provide a simple way to interact with the data sent to and from the client.

1. The Request Object

The request object in Flask is used to access all the data sent from the client during an HTTP request. It allows you to access the HTTP method (GET, POST, PUT, DELETE), form data, query parameters, headers, and cookies.

Here are some common ways to use the request object:

Accessing URL parameters (query strings): If a client sends a GET request to /search?q=flask, you can access the value of q using request.args.get():

python

Copy

```
from flask import request

@app.route('/search')
def search():
    query = request.args.get('q')  # Access query parameter 'q'
    return f'Searching for: {query}'
```

- In this example, if the URL is /search?q=flask, the response will be "Searching for: flask".

Accessing form data (for POST requests): When handling POST requests with form data, you can use request.form.get() to access the data sent in the request body:

python

41

Copy

```
@app.route('/submit', methods=['POST'])
def submit():
    name = request.form.get('name')
    return f'Hello, {name}!'
```

- If the client sends a form with the field name=John, the response will be "Hello, John!".

Accessing JSON data: When working with JSON data (often used in APIs), Flask makes it easy to access the body of the request with request.get_json(). This method returns the parsed JSON data as a Python dictionary.

python

Copy

```
@app.route('/json', methods=['POST'])
def handle_json():
    data = request.get_json()  # Parse JSON body
    name = data.get('name')
    return f'Hello, {name}!'
```

- If the client sends a POST request with a JSON body like {"name": "John"}, the response will be "Hello, John!".

2. The Response Object

The response object is used to generate the response that will be sent back to the client. You can manually construct a response using the Flask instance's make_response() method or simply return a string or JSON object directly from a view function.

Here are some examples of constructing different types of responses:

Returning a String: Flask automatically converts a string return value into an HTTP response with a status code of 200:

42

python

Copy

```python
@app.route('/')
def home():
    return 'Welcome to the API!'
```

- **Returning JSON:** Flask provides a jsonify() function that turns Python dictionaries into JSON responses:

python

Copy

```python
from flask import jsonify


@app.route('/user')
def user():
    user_data = {'id': 1, 'name': 'John Doe'}
    return jsonify(user_data)
```

- This will return a response with the content type application/json and the JSON representation of the user_data dictionary.

Setting Custom Status Codes: You can customize the status code of the response by returning a tuple with the response body and status code:

python

Copy

```python
@app.route('/create', methods=['POST'])
def create():
    return 'Resource created', 201  # 201 Created status code
```

- In this case, the server will respond with the message "Resource created" and a 201 Created HTTP status code, indicating that a new resource was successfully created.

43

Setting Response Headers: You can also set custom response headers using the response.headers attribute:

python

Copy

```
@app.route('/custom-header')
def custom_header():
    response = make_response('Custom header set!')
    response.headers['X-Custom-Header'] = 'Value'
    return response
```

- Here, the response will include an additional header X-Custom-Header with the value "Value".

3.3 Handling JSON Data in Flask APIs

JSON (JavaScript Object Notation) is the standard format for sending data in RESTful APIs. Flask provides a simple way to work with JSON data, both when receiving it from a client and sending it back in the response.

1. Receiving JSON Data

When a client sends JSON data in the body of a request, Flask can easily parse it using request.get_json(). This method will parse the incoming JSON and return it as a Python dictionary.

Here's an example of how to handle a POST request with JSON data:

python

Copy

```
from flask import request
```

```python
@app.route('/create', methods=['POST'])
def create():
    data = request.get_json()  # Parse incoming JSON data
    name = data.get('name')
    age = data.get('age')
    return f'Name: {name}, Age: {age}'
```

If the client sends a request with a JSON body like this:

json

Copy

```json
{
  "name": "John Doe",
  "age": 30
}
```

The response would be "Name: John Doe, Age: 30".

2. Sending JSON Data

To send JSON data as a response, use Flask's jsonify() function. jsonify() takes a Python dictionary or list and converts it into a JSON response with the appropriate content type (application/json).

python

Copy

```python
from flask import jsonify

@app.route('/user')
def get_user():
```

```
user_data = {'id': 1, 'name': 'John Doe'}
return jsonify(user_data)
```

This will return the following response with the content type application/json:

json
Copy
```
{
  "id": 1,
  "name": "John Doe"
}
```

3. Handling JSON Errors

When working with JSON data, errors can sometimes occur, such as when the incoming data is malformed or missing required fields. Flask provides a way to handle such errors and return meaningful error messages.

Here's an example of handling errors when the client sends invalid JSON:

python
Copy
```
from flask import jsonify, request

@app.route('/create', methods=['POST'])
def create():
    try:
        data = request.get_json()
        if not data:
            raise ValueError('No JSON data provided')
```

```
    # Handle the data...
    return jsonify({'message': 'Data received successfully'})
except Exception as e:
    return jsonify({'error': str(e)}), 400  # Return 400 Bad Request with error message
```

In this example, if the client sends invalid JSON or no JSON at all, Flask will respond with a 400 Bad Request status code and a detailed error message in the response body.

With these foundational Flask concepts, you are now equipped to handle basic request and response interactions in your API.

3.4 Flask's Template Engine: Jinja2

While Flask is primarily known for its simplicity in building web applications and APIs, it also comes with a powerful template engine called **Jinja2**. This template engine is essential when you need to generate dynamic HTML or other text-based formats based on data. In the context of API development, however, Jinja2 may not be used as often since APIs primarily return JSON, XML, or other data formats instead of HTML. Nevertheless, it's important to understand the fundamentals of Jinja2, as it can come in handy for building views in web applications or when you need to render templates dynamically in your API.

1. What is Jinja2?

Jinja2 is a modern and designer-friendly templating engine for Python. It's used to generate text-based formats (such as HTML or XML) by combining templates with data. In Flask, Jinja2 is integrated seamlessly, allowing you to generate dynamic content using template files.

47

A **template** is essentially a file that contains placeholders for data. The placeholders are marked with specific syntax, and when the template is rendered, those placeholders are replaced with actual values.

2. Basic Jinja2 Syntax

Jinja2 uses special syntax for placeholders:

- **Variables:** {{ variable_name }}
- **Control structures:** {% for item in list %} ... {% endfor %}, {% if condition %} ... {% endif %}

For example, you could create a template to display a list of users:

html
Copy

```
<ul>
  {% for user in users %}
    <li>{{ user.name }} - {{ user.email }}</li>
  {% endfor %}
</ul>
```

Here, users is a list of objects, and name and email are attributes of each user. The for loop iterates over the list, and each user's data is dynamically injected into the HTML.

3. Using Jinja2 in Flask

While Flask's main focus is API development, it's often used for full-stack web applications where dynamic HTML rendering is needed. Flask automatically uses Jinja2 for rendering HTML templates in views. For example, you might render an HTML page with dynamic content like so:

python
48

Copy

```
from flask import render_template

@app.route('/users')
def show_users():
    users = [{'name': 'John Doe', 'email': 'john@example.com'}, {'name': 'Jane Smith', 'email': 'jane@example.com'}]
    return render_template('users.html', users=users)
```

Here, render_template() renders the users.html template, passing the users list into the template for dynamic rendering.

4. When is Jinja2 Useful for APIs?

Although Jinja2 is typically used for rendering HTML, it can also be useful for APIs in specific scenarios. For example, you might want to return a dynamically generated HTML page in response to a certain API request or generate an email body from a template. In these cases, Flask's integration with Jinja2 can save you from manually string-building the response, making your code cleaner and more maintainable.

In an API context, you might use Jinja2 to:

- Generate an HTML email body and send it via SMTP.
- Create dynamic content for documentation or reports.
- Customize the format of responses for browsers that accept HTML (like when returning an HTML form instead of JSON).

In a typical Flask API, however, you'll more often use JSON responses rather than rendering HTML with Jinja2.

49

3.5 Building and Testing Simple API Endpoints

In this section, we'll explore how to build and test basic API endpoints using Flask. By the end of this, you should be comfortable creating simple routes, handling HTTP methods like GET, POST, and DELETE, and testing your endpoints to ensure they work as expected.

1. Building Simple Endpoints

Flask makes it easy to build API endpoints by defining routes that handle specific HTTP methods. Let's create a simple API with a few endpoints:

Creating a GET endpoint:

python
Copy

```
@app.route('/greet', methods=['GET'])
def greet():
    return 'Hello, API!'
```

This is a basic GET request handler that returns a string when the /greet endpoint is accessed.

Creating a POST endpoint:

Let's define a POST endpoint where clients can send data. The following example allows users to send their name in the request body, and it will return a personalized greeting.

python
Copy

```
@app.route('/greet', methods=['POST'])
```

```python
def greet_post():
    data = request.get_json()
    name = data.get('name')
    return jsonify({'message': f'Hello, {name}!'})
```

In this case:

- The endpoint /greet accepts POST requests.
- The request.get_json() method is used to parse the incoming JSON data.
- The name field from the JSON body is used to create a personalized greeting.

Creating a DELETE endpoint:

Let's say we want to delete a user from our API. A DELETE endpoint would be useful in this case:

python

Copy

```python
@app.route('/users/<int:user_id>', methods=['DELETE'])
def delete_user(user_id):
    # Here we would delete the user from the database or data structure
    return jsonify({'message': f'User {user_id} has been deleted'}), 200
```

This DELETE endpoint accepts a URL parameter (user_id) and simulates deleting a user.

2. Testing API Endpoints

Testing your API endpoints ensures that your routes work as expected. Flask provides a built-in test client that allows you to simulate requests to your application without needing an actual browser.

Here's how you can test the endpoints we've defined using Flask's test client:

Testing GET endpoint:

python
Copy
```
def test_greet_get():
    with app.test_client() as client:
        response = client.get('/greet')
        assert response.data == b'Hello, API!'
```

In this example, we use client.get() to send a GET request to /greet and check that the response matches the expected output.

Testing POST endpoint:

python
Copy
```
def test_greet_post():
    with app.test_client() as client:
        response = client.post('/greet', json={'name': 'John'})
        assert response.json == {'message': 'Hello, John!'}
```

Here, client.post() is used to send a POST request to /greet with JSON data. We then check that the returned JSON matches the expected message.

Testing DELETE endpoint:

python
Copy
```
def test_delete_user():
```

```
with app.test_client() as client:
    response = client.delete('/users/1')
    assert response.json == {'message': 'User 1 has been deleted'}
```

In this case, client.delete() sends a DELETE request to /users/1, and we check that the response contains the expected confirmation message.

3. Running the Tests

To run the tests, you can use the pytest testing framework. Simply install pytest and run the tests using the following command:

Copy
```
pip install pytest
pytest
```

This will automatically discover and run all the test functions defined in your Flask application.

3.6 Flask Blueprints for API Organization

As your API grows, you'll likely end up with a large number of routes, which can make your application difficult to manage. To keep your code organized and modular, Flask provides a feature called **Blueprints**.

A **Blueprint** in Flask allows you to organize routes and views into separate components, each with its own set of related routes, templates, and static files. You can then register these blueprints with the main Flask application.

1. What are Blueprints?

Blueprints allow you to define routes in separate files or modules, which can be reused and registered in the main application. This helps break up the application into smaller, manageable parts and keeps the codebase clean.

Here's an example of how to create and use blueprints:

Creating a Blueprint:

```python
Copy
from flask import Blueprint

# Create a Blueprint object
user_bp = Blueprint('user', __name__)

# Define routes for the blueprint
@user_bp.route('/users')
def get_users():
    return 'List of users'

@user_bp.route('/users/<int:user_id>')
def get_user(user_id):
    return f'User with ID {user_id}'
```

In this example, we define a blueprint named user_bp with two routes: /users and /users/<user_id>.

Registering a Blueprint with the Flask App:

python

Copy

```
from flask import Flask

app = Flask(__name__)

# Register the blueprint with the app
app.register_blueprint(user_bp, url_prefix='/api')
```

Here, we register the user_bp blueprint with the Flask application and specify a url_prefix of /api. This means the blueprint's routes will be accessible under the /api path (e.g., /api/users).

2. Benefits of Using Blueprints

- **Modular Code:** Blueprints allow you to group related routes into separate modules. For example, you could create separate blueprints for users, authentication, and posts.
- **Reusability:** You can reuse blueprints in different projects or environments without needing to rewrite code.
- **Cleaner Structure:** Blueprints help organize your code into logical sections, making it easier to maintain and extend.

3.7 Summary & What's Next

In this chapter, we explored the foundational concepts of Flask, focusing on building simple APIs, handling requests and responses, and organizing routes using Flask's blueprint system. Here's a summary of what we've covered:

- **Flask Architecture:** We reviewed the core components of Flask, including the Flask instance, routes, views, and the request/response cycle.
- **Working with Flask's Request and Response Objects:** We learned how to access request data (e.g., URL parameters, form data, JSON) and generate responses (e.g., strings, JSON, status codes).
- **Handling JSON Data:** We explored how Flask handles JSON data, both for incoming requests and outgoing responses.
- **Building and Testing API Endpoints:** We created simple API endpoints using Flask and tested them using Flask's built-in test client.
- **Flask Blueprints:** We discussed how to use Flask Blueprints to organize your API into modular components for better maintainability and scalability.

In the next chapter, we will build on these concepts by diving into more advanced topics such as working with databases, authentication, and implementing error handling to make your API robust and production-ready.

Chapter 4: Building Scalable APIs with Flask

4.1 What Is Scalability in API Design?

Scalability in API design refers to the ability of an API to handle increasing numbers of requests, users, and data without degrading performance. As your API grows in popularity or usage, it's crucial that the architecture can handle higher loads efficiently. This is particularly important when your application expands or when dealing with high traffic from many clients, each making requests concurrently.

There are two main types of scalability to consider when designing APIs:

1. Horizontal Scaling (Scaling Out)

Horizontal scaling involves adding more servers to distribute the load across multiple machines. This is the most common method used in cloud-based applications and is essential for handling increased traffic. By deploying your Flask application on multiple servers, you can increase your system's capacity to handle more requests in parallel.

Example: If your application is hosted on a single server and that server is receiving too many requests, you can deploy your app on multiple servers. Load balancers distribute the requests evenly across these servers.

2. Vertical Scaling (Scaling Up)

Vertical scaling involves upgrading your existing server with more resources, such as adding more CPU power, memory, or disk space. While this can be effective for some applications, vertical scaling has limits because a single server can only grow so much before reaching its physical limits.

Example: If your current server's CPU is being maxed out, you might increase the server's processing power or memory. However, this approach may not scale efficiently in the long term compared to horizontal scaling.

3. Why Scalability Matters

APIs that are not designed to scale efficiently may experience slow response times, downtime, or errors under heavy traffic. The key to successful scalability is designing your API to distribute the load across multiple resources (whether that's more servers or optimized code) and ensuring that it can handle spikes in demand.

4. Key Aspects of Scalable API Design

- **Load Distribution:** Distributing traffic efficiently across servers and database resources ensures that no single server is overloaded.
- **Caching:** Caching frequently accessed data reduces the need for repeated database queries and improves response times.
- **Asynchronous Processing:** Offloading long-running tasks (like sending emails or processing data) to background workers prevents delays in serving API requests.
- **Database Scaling:** Techniques like database replication, sharding, and indexing improve the scalability of the database layer.

4.2 Flask and Performance Optimization: Key Strategies

Optimizing Flask for performance involves addressing various factors that can impact the responsiveness and efficiency of the API. By focusing on both application-level and server-level performance, you can ensure your Flask API handles increased traffic smoothly.

1. Minimize Application Overhead

Flask's minimalistic nature gives you the flexibility to design your application in a way that minimizes unnecessary overhead. Here are some key strategies:

- **Use Flask's Built-in Features Wisely:** While Flask is lightweight, it's important to avoid unnecessary dependencies. Only import the modules you need, and be mindful of using external libraries that may introduce performance bottlenecks.
- **Optimize Request Handling:** Ensure that your views are designed efficiently. Avoid complex operations or database queries that can slow down the response time. Limit the amount of logic performed within route handlers and offload heavy computations when possible.

2. Caching to Improve Response Times

Caching is one of the most effective ways to speed up your API. By storing the results of expensive operations or frequent queries, you can serve them faster for subsequent requests without redoing the work.

In-Memory Caching: Use in-memory caching systems like **Redis** or **Memcached** to cache the results of API calls or database queries. Flask can easily integrate with these tools via extensions like Flask-Caching.

Example:

python

Copy

```
from flask_caching import Cache

app = Flask(__name__)
cache = Cache(app, config={'CACHE_TYPE': 'simple'})

@app.route('/data')
@cache.cached(timeout=60)  # Cache response for 60 seconds
```

59

```python
def get_data():
    return jsonify({'data': 'expensive to compute'})
```

- **HTTP Caching:** Flask supports HTTP caching mechanisms like **ETags** and **Cache-Control** headers. These can be used to instruct clients to cache responses locally, reducing load on your server.

3. Use Asynchronous and Background Processing

By offloading time-consuming tasks to background workers, you can avoid blocking the main application thread, allowing the API to serve other requests while the background tasks are being processed. This is especially useful for tasks like sending emails, processing files, or handling data transformations.

Celery: Flask works well with **Celery**, a distributed task queue that can be used to handle background jobs. Celery allows you to delegate long-running tasks to workers that operate asynchronously, improving the API's responsiveness.

Example:

python

Copy

```python
from celery import Celery

app = Flask(__name__)
celery = Celery(app.name, broker='redis://localhost:6379/0')

@celery.task
def send_email():
    # Simulate sending an email
    pass

@app.route('/send_email')
def send_email_route():
```

60

```
send_email.apply_async()  # Send email asynchronously
return 'Email is being sent!'
```

4. Database Optimization

Database queries can often be a bottleneck in an API. Flask's ORM (Object-Relational Mapping) tool, **SQLAlchemy**, can help optimize database operations. Here are some best practices for improving database performance:

- **Use Indexing:** Index frequently queried columns to speed up search operations.
- **Database Pooling:** Use a connection pool to manage database connections efficiently. This reduces the overhead of establishing new connections for every request.
- **Optimize Queries:** Write efficient queries by limiting the amount of data retrieved and using joins or subqueries where appropriate.

5. Profiling and Monitoring

To understand where performance bottlenecks lie in your application, use profiling tools to monitor and analyze your API's performance.

- **Flask-Profiler:** Use Flask-Profiler to measure how long each route takes to process requests and identify slow areas.
- **New Relic or Datadog:** These third-party services provide real-time application performance monitoring, allowing you to monitor Flask's performance in production.

6. Optimize Static Assets

Even in API development, static files like images, CSS, and JavaScript may be served occasionally (e.g., in admin panels or documentation). Make sure these assets are compressed and served via a content delivery network (CDN) to reduce load time.

4.3 Scaling Flask APIs with Load Balancers

Scaling Flask APIs often requires distributing traffic across multiple instances to ensure high availability and handle growing traffic volumes. This is where **load balancers** come into play.

1. What is a Load Balancer?

A load balancer is a device or service that distributes incoming network traffic across multiple servers. The goal is to ensure no single server is overwhelmed with too much traffic and that resources are used optimally. Load balancers help ensure your application can scale horizontally, providing reliability and fault tolerance.

2. Load Balancer Architecture

In a typical architecture for Flask applications, you would deploy multiple instances of your Flask app across different servers or containers. A load balancer sits in front of these instances and routes incoming requests to the appropriate server. This ensures that the load is balanced and that no single server bears too much traffic.

Here's a simplified illustration:

- **Clients** send requests to the load balancer.
- **Load Balancer** distributes requests to the available Flask instances (running on separate servers).
- **Flask Instances** process the requests and return responses to the clients.

3. Load Balancing Strategies

There are several strategies load balancers can use to distribute traffic across servers:

- **Round Robin:** This is the simplest load balancing method, where each incoming request is sent to the next server in the list, and the cycle repeats. While this works well for uniform traffic loads, it may not be ideal if servers have different capacities.

- **Least Connections:** The load balancer sends requests to the server with the fewest active connections. This method is particularly useful when there are servers with varying processing capabilities.
- **IP Hash:** The load balancer directs requests from the same IP address to the same server, which is useful for session persistence.

4. Setting Up a Load Balancer for Flask

There are many tools available for setting up a load balancer for Flask applications. Some popular ones include **Nginx**, **HAProxy**, and **AWS Elastic Load Balancer**.

Here's a basic example using **Nginx** as a load balancer to distribute traffic between multiple Flask instances:

1. Install and configure Nginx on your server.
2. Set up multiple instances of your Flask app (either on different servers or containers).
3. Configure Nginx to distribute requests among these instances:

nginx

Copy

```
http {
  upstream flask_backend {
    server 192.168.1.101:5000;
    server 192.168.1.102:5000;
  }

  server {
    location / {
      proxy_pass http://flask_backend;
```

In this configuration, Nginx will distribute incoming traffic between the two Flask instances running on different servers.

5. Benefits of Load Balancing

- **Increased Availability:** If one server goes down, the load balancer can automatically route traffic to other healthy servers.
- **Better Performance:** By distributing the traffic, load balancers help prevent any single server from becoming overwhelmed, improving overall application performance.
- **Scalability:** Load balancing makes it easy to scale your application horizontally by simply adding more servers to the pool.

6. Managing Sticky Sessions

In some cases, you may need to maintain a session for a user across requests. This is called a "sticky session." Many load balancers support sticky sessions, which ensure that a user's requests are always sent to the same server.

This can be achieved using session cookies or IP hashing, which we mentioned earlier. Sticky sessions are useful for APIs that require user authentication or need to track state across requests.

4.4 Caching Strategies for Flask APIs

Caching is a crucial performance optimization technique for APIs, especially when dealing with high traffic and complex database queries. By storing the results of expensive operations in a cache, you can avoid recalculating the same data for every request, significantly reducing response times and decreasing load on your backend systems.

1. What Is Caching?

Caching involves storing copies of data (or results of computations) in a temporary storage layer called a cache. The cached data can be quickly accessed for subsequent requests, avoiding the need for repeated calculations or database queries. There are various types of caching strategies you can use in Flask to enhance performance:

- **Memory Caching:** This is typically the fastest form of caching. It stores data in memory (RAM) on the same server running your application. This can be done using tools like **Flask-Caching** with **Redis** or **Memcached**.
- **Distributed Caching:** In a distributed system, you might use an external cache service like **Redis** or **Memcached** to store cached data across multiple servers. This enables the cache to be shared among multiple Flask application instances.

2. Flask-Caching with Redis

Flask-Caching is a Flask extension that makes it easy to implement caching in your application. Redis is a popular caching tool that can store and retrieve data extremely fast. Here's how to implement caching with Flask and Redis.

Step 1: Install Flask-Caching and Redis First, you need to install the necessary packages:

bash

Copy

```
pip install Flask-Caching redis
```

Step 2: Set up Flask-Caching with Redis Now, you can set up Flask-Caching with Redis in your Flask application:

python

Copy

```
from flask import Flask, jsonify
from flask_caching import Cache

app = Flask(__name__)
app.config['CACHE_TYPE'] = 'redis'
app.config['CACHE_REDIS_URL'] = 'redis://localhost:6379/0'
cache = Cache(app)

@app.route('/data')
@cache.cached(timeout=60)  # Cache this endpoint for 60 seconds
def get_data():
    # Simulate an expensive operation
    data = {'value': 'This is expensive data'}
    return jsonify(data)
```

In this example:

- The @cache.cached() decorator caches the response of the /data endpoint for 60 seconds.
- Redis is used as the caching backend. This means the data will be stored in the Redis cache and served to clients until the cache expires.

Step 3: Test Your Cache After running the Flask app and visiting the /data endpoint, you will notice that the response time is very quick, especially for subsequent requests. The cached response will be returned, and the expensive operation will not be re-executed for every request.

3. Cache Invalidation

One of the challenges of caching is cache invalidation. When your data changes (e.g., a user's information is updated), you need to ensure that the cache is refreshed to reflect these changes.

Example: If you update user information, you might want to clear the cache for any routes related to users.

python
Copy

```
@cache.delete('get_data')
def update_user_data():
    # Update user data in the database
    pass
```

Here, we use @cache.delete() to delete the cached data associated with the get_data endpoint when user data is updated.

4. Types of Cache

- **Full Response Caching:** Cache the entire response of an endpoint. This is useful when the response does not change often and can be served to all users.
- **Partial Caching (Data Caching):** Cache only specific data rather than the entire response. For example, if you have a list of users and some users rarely change, you can cache only the users that don't change often and serve updated ones from the database.

5. Benefits of Caching

- **Faster Response Times:** Reduces the time it takes to return a response by serving precomputed or pre-fetched data.
- **Reduced Server Load:** Reduces the number of requests that hit your database or application server, freeing up resources for other tasks.
- **Scalability:** Caching helps you handle more requests by serving data without needing to recompute or re-fetch it from the database.

4.5 Optimizing Flask's Database Integration for Scale

Flask's database integration is often handled through an ORM (Object-Relational Mapping) tool like **SQLAlchemy**. While ORMs provide a convenient abstraction for working with databases, they can sometimes be inefficient, especially when dealing with large datasets or complex queries. Optimizing Flask's database integration for scalability ensures that your API can handle high traffic while maintaining fast response times.

1. Use Database Indexing

Indexes are one of the most effective ways to speed up database queries. An index is a data structure that improves the speed of data retrieval operations on a database table. When your Flask app interacts with the database, queries that involve indexed columns will run much faster.

Example:

python
Copy
```
class User(db.Model):
    id = db.Column(db.Integer, primary_key=True)
    username = db.Column(db.String(80), index=True)  # Indexing username column
```

68

```
email = db.Column(db.String(120), unique=True)
```

Here, the username column is indexed, which will improve query performance when filtering or searching by username.

2. Use Query Optimization

When building queries in Flask, especially when using SQLAlchemy, it's important to write efficient queries that avoid unnecessary operations:

Avoid SELECT : Instead of selecting all columns from a table, only select the columns you need.

python

Copy

```
users = User.query.with_entities(User.id, User.username).all()
```

- **Limit the Number of Results:** For large datasets, always implement pagination or limit the number of results returned.

  python

  Copy

  ```
  users = User.query.paginate(page=1, per_page=20)
  ```

- **Lazy Loading vs. Eager Loading:** By default, SQLAlchemy uses lazy loading, which means related objects are loaded when they are accessed. However, this can lead to unnecessary queries being executed. To avoid this, use eager loading to load related objects in a single query.

  python

  Copy

  ```
  from sqlalchemy.orm import joinedload
  ```

```
users = User.query.options(joinedload(User.profile)).all()
```

69

3. Database Connection Pooling

Flask uses SQLAlchemy for ORM, and by default, it opens a new database connection for each request. This can become a bottleneck under high traffic. To mitigate this, enable database connection pooling, which reuses database connections rather than opening new ones.

python
Copy
```
app.config['SQLALCHEMY_POOL_SIZE'] = 10  # Set the maximum number of connections in the pool
app.config['SQLALCHEMY_POOL_TIMEOUT'] = 30  # Timeout after 30 seconds if no connection is available
```

4. Database Sharding and Replication

For large-scale applications, you may want to use **sharding** and **replication** to distribute the load. Sharding involves breaking up large datasets into smaller, more manageable pieces across different databases. Replication involves creating copies of the database for read-heavy applications to distribute the query load.

5. Use a Read-Write Split

In many production applications, database reads are more frequent than writes. You can optimize performance by setting up a **read-write split**, where read queries are sent to replica databases, while write operations go to the primary database.

python
Copy
```
app.config['SQLALCHEMY_DATABASE_URI'] =
'postgres://user:pass@primary-db-url:5432/dbname'
app.config['SQLALCHEMY_BINDS'] = {
```

'read': 'postgres://user:pass@replica-db-url:5432/dbname'

}

By directing read operations to replica databases, you reduce the load on the primary database, improving scalability.

4.6 Asynchronous Tasks and Background Jobs in Flask

As your Flask application grows, you may need to handle long-running tasks such as sending emails, processing large files, or interacting with external APIs. These tasks can block the main thread of your application, resulting in delayed responses. To address this, Flask allows you to implement **asynchronous tasks** and **background jobs** using external libraries like **Celery**.

1. What Is Asynchronous Processing?

Asynchronous processing allows tasks to run independently of the main application thread. When a task is offloaded to a background worker, the API can immediately respond to the client without waiting for the task to complete.

2. Setting Up Celery with Flask

Celery is a popular distributed task queue that works well with Flask. To get started with Celery, you need to install it along with a message broker, such as **Redis** or **RabbitMQ**.

bash
Copy
```
pip install Celery redis
```

Here's how you can set up Celery in your Flask app:

Step 1: Configure Celery

python

Copy

```python
from celery import Celery

app = Flask(__name__)

# Configure Celery with Flask's app settings
app.config['CELERY_BROKER_URL'] = 'redis://localhost:6379/0'
celery = Celery(app.name, broker=app.config['CELERY_BROKER_URL'])
celery.conf.update(app.config)
```

Step 2: Define a Task Define a Celery task that runs in the background:

python

Copy

```python
@celery.task
def send_email(email_address):
    # Simulate sending an email
    print(f'Sending email to {email_address}')
```

Step 3: Call the Task Asynchronously You can now call the task asynchronously from your Flask route:

python

Copy

```python
@app.route('/send_email/<email_address>')
```

```
def send_email_route(email_address):
    send_email.apply_async(args=[email_address])
    return 'Email is being sent!'
```

Step 4: Running the Celery Worker To process background tasks, you need to run a Celery worker in a separate terminal:

bash
Copy

```
celery -A app.celery worker
```

Now, when you visit /send_email/<email_address>, Flask will immediately respond, and Celery will handle the background task of sending the email.

3. Benefits of Asynchronous Tasks

- **Improved User Experience:** Offloading long-running tasks ensures that the API can respond quickly to users.
- **Better Resource Management:** Instead of blocking the main thread, background tasks run in the background, utilizing worker processes or threads.
- **Scalability:** Asynchronous processing allows you to scale background workers independently of the API servers.

4.7 Summary & What's Next

In this chapter, we explored strategies for scaling Flask APIs to handle increased load and traffic:

- **Caching Strategies:** We covered the importance of caching for reducing response times and database load. Using tools like Redis, we discussed caching responses, managing cache expiration, and cache invalidation.
- **Optimizing Flask's Database Integration for Scale:** We reviewed techniques for optimizing database performance, including indexing, query optimization, and connection pooling, as well as strategies like read-write splitting and database sharding.
- **Asynchronous Tasks and Background Jobs:** We learned how to offload long-running tasks using Celery, enabling Flask to handle other requests without delays.

In the next chapter, we will explore securing your Flask APIs, focusing on authentication, authorization, and best practices for protecting sensitive data and ensuring the integrity of your API.

Chapter 5: Ensuring API Security

5.1 Common API Security Threats

API security is a critical aspect of API development, especially when sensitive data is being transferred between clients and servers. APIs are often exposed to various security risks and threats that could compromise data integrity, user privacy, and overall system performance. Understanding and mitigating these risks is essential to building a robust, secure API.

Here are some of the most common API security threats you should be aware of:

1. Injection Attacks (SQL, Command, etc.)

Injection attacks occur when an attacker is able to inject malicious data (such as SQL queries or system commands) into an API request, leading to unauthorized access or data manipulation. One of the most common forms of injection is **SQL injection**, where malicious SQL code is inserted into a query that interacts with the database.

How to mitigate:

- Use **parameterized queries** or **prepared statements** to prevent SQL injection.
- Validate and sanitize user input before using it in queries.

2. Cross-Site Scripting (XSS)

Cross-Site Scripting (XSS) occurs when an attacker injects malicious scripts (often JavaScript) into content that is returned to users. If a malicious script is executed in a user's browser, it can steal sensitive data, hijack sessions, or perform other harmful actions.

How to mitigate:

- **Escape output** before rendering it to prevent scripts from being executed.
- Use tools like **Content Security Policy (CSP)** headers to restrict the types of content loaded by your API.

3. Cross-Site Request Forgery (CSRF)

CSRF is an attack where an attacker tricks a user into performing actions without their consent, such as making unwanted requests or changing sensitive data. This usually happens when an attacker lures a user to visit a malicious website that performs actions on a different website on which the user is logged in.

How to mitigate:

- Use anti-CSRF tokens for sensitive actions.
- Implement strict **SameSite cookies** policies to restrict cross-origin requests.

4. Broken Authentication and Session Management

APIs are often vulnerable to attacks if authentication and session management are not properly implemented. Weak password policies, insufficient session expiration, and improperly handled authentication tokens can make APIs susceptible to impersonation and unauthorized access.

How to mitigate:

- Use strong **password policies** and multi-factor authentication (MFA).
- Use **secure authentication tokens** (such as JWT or OAuth) and ensure tokens are encrypted and stored securely.
- Implement **token expiration** and **revocation** mechanisms to limit the lifespan of authentication tokens.

5. Insecure Direct Object References (IDOR)

Insecure Direct Object References (IDOR) occur when attackers can access or modify objects (such as files or database records) by manipulating input parameters, such as IDs in URLs. If not properly validated, an attacker may gain unauthorized access to sensitive data.

How to mitigate:

- Always **validate user access** and ensure that users can only access objects they are authorized to interact with.
- Use **indirect references** for resources (e.g., hashed or random tokens) instead of predictable IDs in URLs.

6. Denial of Service (DoS) and Distributed Denial of Service (DDoS) Attacks

DoS and DDoS attacks aim to overwhelm your API with excessive traffic, making it unavailable to legitimate users. These attacks exploit the server's resources, leading to degraded performance or complete downtime.

How to mitigate:

- Implement **rate limiting** to restrict the number of requests a user can make within a certain time frame.
- Use **CDNs** and **WAFs (Web Application Firewalls)** to filter malicious traffic and absorb traffic spikes.

7. Sensitive Data Exposure

Exposing sensitive data through API responses, either unintentionally or through vulnerabilities, can lead to severe privacy and security breaches. This includes exposing personal information, financial data, or system credentials in API responses.

How to mitigate:

- **Encrypt sensitive data** both in transit (using HTTPS) and at rest (using database encryption).
- Avoid exposing sensitive data in API responses unless absolutely necessary, and always follow the **principle of least privilege** when granting access to sensitive resources.

8. Insufficient Logging and Monitoring

A lack of proper logging and monitoring of API requests can make it difficult to detect malicious activities or attacks. Without monitoring, it becomes much harder to respond to potential breaches in a timely manner.

How to mitigate:

- Implement detailed **logging** for all API requests and responses, ensuring sensitive information is not logged.
- Set up **monitoring** and **alerting systems** to detect unusual or suspicious activity.

5.2 Flask Security Best Practices

While Flask is a lightweight and flexible framework, securing your Flask API requires implementing best practices to protect against common threats. Here are some best practices to ensure your Flask API is secure:

1. Use HTTPS (SSL/TLS)

Always serve your API over **HTTPS** to ensure data is encrypted in transit. HTTPS helps protect sensitive information from being intercepted during communication between the client and the server.

How to implement: Use a trusted **SSL/TLS certificate** and configure your Flask application to only serve requests over HTTPS.

python
Copy

```python
if __name__ == '__main__':
    app.run(ssl_context=('cert.pem', 'key.pem'))
```

2. Secure Authentication Tokens (JWT)

When using authentication tokens, **JSON Web Tokens (JWT)** are a popular choice. JWTs are compact, URL-safe tokens that can securely transmit information between parties. To ensure security:

- Use a strong **signing algorithm** like HS256 or RS256 when creating the token.
- Set **expiration times** for tokens to limit their lifespan.
- Use **secure storage** for tokens, such as **HTTP-only cookies**.

Example:

python
Copy

```python
import jwt
from datetime import datetime, timedelta

# Generate JWT Token
def generate_jwt(payload, secret_key):
    expiration = datetime.utcnow() + timedelta(hours=1)
    payload.update({'exp': expiration})
    token = jwt.encode(payload, secret_key, algorithm='HS256')
    return token
```

3. Protect Against SQL Injection

When interacting with databases in Flask, it's crucial to protect against **SQL injection** attacks. Always use **parameterized queries** or **ORMs** like SQLAlchemy, which automatically handles query parameters safely.

Example with SQLAlchemy (using ORM):

python
Copy
```
user = db.session.query(User).filter_by(id=user_id).first()
```

4. Enable Cross-Origin Resource Sharing (CORS)

Cross-Origin Resource Sharing (CORS) is a security feature implemented by browsers to control how resources on a server can be requested from another domain. Flask can handle CORS with the **Flask-CORS** extension.

Example:

bash
Copy
```
pip install flask-cors
```

python
Copy
```
from flask_cors import CORS
app = Flask(__name__)
CORS(app)
```

This allows you to specify which domains are allowed to access your API, thus preventing unauthorized cross-origin requests.

5. Implement Rate Limiting

Rate limiting restricts how many requests a client can make in a specified period, helping to prevent abuse or DoS attacks. Flask can implement rate limiting using extensions like **Flask-Limiter**.

Example:

bash

Copy

```
pip install Flask-Limiter
```

python

Copy

```
from flask_limiter import Limiter
limiter = Limiter(app)

@app.route("/some_resource")
@limiter.limit("5 per minute")
def some_resource():
    return "This resource is rate-limited."
```

This example allows a maximum of 5 requests per minute to the /some_resource endpoint.

6. Secure Session Management

Flask uses secure cookies to store session data. To ensure secure session management:

- Set **secure cookie attributes** to ensure cookies are only transmitted over HTTPS (secure=True).
- Use **session expiration** and **logout functionality** to invalidate sessions after a certain time.

Example:

python

Copy

```
from flask import session

app.config['SECRET_KEY'] = 'your_secret_key'
app.config['SESSION_COOKIE_SECURE'] = True  # Only use cookies over HTTPS
```

7. Sanitize User Inputs

Always sanitize user input to avoid malicious data being processed by your API. Flask has built-in mechanisms to help validate and sanitize form data, but additional manual checks might be required for custom inputs.

5.3 Implementing Authentication and Authorization (JWT, OAuth)

Authentication and authorization are critical parts of API security. They ensure that only legitimate users can access the API and that users only have access to the resources they're authorized to use. Two common approaches for securing APIs are **JWT (JSON Web Tokens)** and **OAuth**.

1. JSON Web Tokens (JWT)

JWT is a popular method for handling authentication in modern APIs. It is compact and self-contained, which means all the necessary information (such as user ID, roles, and expiration time) is embedded in the token itself. JWTs are signed with a secret key, ensuring their integrity.

How JWT works:

- **Authentication:** The user sends their credentials (e.g., username and password) to the API.
- **Token Generation:** If the credentials are valid, the server generates a JWT and sends it back to the client.
- **Authorization:** For subsequent requests, the client includes the JWT in the request header, and the server validates the token before granting access.

Example of JWT Authentication in Flask:

python
Copy

```python
from flask import Flask, request, jsonify
import jwt
from datetime import datetime, timedelta

app = Flask(__name__)
SECRET_KEY = 'your_secret_key'

# Function to create JWT token
def create_jwt_token(user_id):
    expiration = datetime.utcnow() + timedelta(hours=1)
    payload = {'user_id': user_id, 'exp': expiration}
    token = jwt.encode(payload, SECRET_KEY, algorithm='HS256')
```

```
    return token

@app.route('/login', methods=['POST'])
def login():
    data = request.json
    username = data.get('username')
    password = data.get('password')
    if username == 'admin' and password == 'password':  # Simplified check
        token = create_jwt_token(username)
        return jsonify({'token': token})
    return jsonify({'error': 'Invalid credentials'}), 401
```

2. OAuth 2.0

OAuth 2.0 is a more comprehensive and flexible authentication framework that allows third-party applications to access user resources without needing to share their credentials. OAuth is commonly used for implementing **Authorization** using an access token.

How OAuth works:

- **Authorization Code Flow:** The user is redirected to an authorization server (e.g., Google or Facebook), where they authorize the application to access their data.
- **Access Token:** The authorization server sends an access token to the client, which can then be used to access the API on behalf of the user.

Example with Flask and OAuth2: You would typically use an OAuth library such as **Authlib** or **Flask-OAuthlib** to implement OAuth.

bash

Copy

```
pip install Authlib
```

python

Copy

```python
from flask import Flask, redirect, url_for
from authlib.integrations.flask_client import OAuth

app = Flask(__name__)
oauth = OAuth(app)

google = oauth.register(
    name='google',
    client_id='GOOGLE_CLIENT_ID',
    client_secret='GOOGLE_CLIENT_SECRET',
    authorize_url='https://accounts.google.com/o/oauth2/auth',
    authorize_params=None,
    access_token_url='https://accounts.google.com/o/oauth2/token',
    refresh_token_url=None,
    client_kwargs={'scope': 'openid profile email'},
)

@app.route('/login')
def login():
    redirect_uri = url_for('auth', _external=True)
    return google.authorize_redirect(redirect_uri)
```

OAuth provides more advanced features such as refresh tokens, scopes, and user consent screens, making it suitable for securing APIs that need third-party authentication.

5.4 Protecting Against SQL Injection and XSS Attacks

SQL injection and Cross-Site Scripting (XSS) are two of the most common and dangerous attacks targeting APIs. These attacks exploit weaknesses in how input is handled, and without proper safeguards, they can lead to data breaches, unauthorized access, and other serious vulnerabilities. Here's how you can protect your Flask API against these attacks:

1. Protecting Against SQL Injection

SQL injection occurs when malicious SQL queries are injected into an API's query string or form data. This allows attackers to manipulate the SQL query, potentially accessing or modifying sensitive data.

How to mitigate SQL injection:

- **Use Parameterized Queries**: This is the most effective way to protect your application from SQL injection. Parameterized queries use placeholders for user input, which ensures that user data is treated as a value and not executable code.

Example using SQLAlchemy (Flask's ORM):

python

Copy

```
from flask import Flask, request

from flask_sqlalchemy import SQLAlchemy


app = Flask(__name__)
```

```python
app.config['SQLALCHEMY_DATABASE_URI'] = 'sqlite:///users.db'

db = SQLAlchemy(app)


class User(db.Model):

    id = db.Column(db.Integer, primary_key=True)

    username = db.Column(db.String(80), unique=True, nullable=False)


@app.route('/user', methods=['GET'])

def get_user():

    username = request.args.get('username')

    user = User.query.filter_by(username=username).first()  # This is safe from SQL injection

    if user:

        return {'username': user.username}, 200

    return {'message': 'User not found'}, 404
```

In this example, the filter_by method of SQLAlchemy uses parameterized queries, ensuring that the user input (username) is treated as data rather than executable SQL code.

- **Avoid Concatenating SQL Queries**: Never concatenate or interpolate user input directly into SQL queries. This makes your application vulnerable to SQL injection.

python

Copy

```
# Vulnerable to SQL injection

query = "SELECT * FROM users WHERE username = '" + user_input + "'"
```

- **Use ORM (Object-Relational Mapping)**: ORM libraries like SQLAlchemy, which are designed to abstract database queries, typically prevent SQL injection by automatically parameterizing queries.

2. Protecting Against XSS (Cross-Site Scripting)

XSS attacks occur when an attacker injects malicious JavaScript code into an API response. If this script is executed by a user's browser, it can steal session cookies, perform actions on behalf of the user, or redirect users to malicious sites.

How to mitigate XSS:

- **Escape Output**: When rendering user input, always ensure that it's escaped to prevent malicious scripts from being executed in the user's browser. Flask's built-in render_template method automatically escapes HTML by default. However, if you're generating HTML manually, make sure to escape any user-provided content.

For example, if you're returning a user's profile information as part of an HTML response:

88

python

Copy

```python
from flask import Flask, render_template


@app.route('/profile')

def profile():

    username = request.args.get('username')

    # Automatically escapes any special characters to prevent XSS

    return render_template('profile.html', username=username)
```

- **Use Content Security Policy (CSP)**: CSP is an HTTP header that helps prevent malicious scripts from executing in the browser. By using CSP, you can specify which domains are allowed to serve content (e.g., scripts, images), effectively blocking malicious scripts from unauthorized sources.

Example CSP header:

python

Copy

```python
@app.after_request

def add_csp_header(response):

    response.headers['Content-Security-Policy'] = "default-src 'self'; script-src 'self';"
```

```
return response
```

- **Validate and Sanitize User Input**: Always validate and sanitize user input before it's used. This includes filtering out harmful characters, such as <, >, and script.

Sanitizing User Input Example:

python

Copy

```python
import re

def sanitize_input(user_input):
    sanitized_input = re.sub(r'<.*?>', '', user_input)  # Remove HTML tags
    return sanitized_input
```

By using these measures, you can prevent SQL injection and XSS attacks, ensuring that your Flask API remains secure.

5.5 Using HTTPS to Secure API Endpoints

One of the most basic yet crucial security measures is serving your API over **HTTPS** (HyperText Transfer Protocol Secure). HTTPS encrypts data in transit, ensuring that sensitive information such as login credentials, user data, and financial transactions cannot be intercepted by malicious actors.

1. Why HTTPS is Critical

- **Encryption**: HTTPS encrypts the data sent between the client and the server, protecting it from interception by third parties.
- **Authentication**: HTTPS ensures that users are communicating with the intended server, preventing man-in-the-middle (MITM) attacks where an attacker intercepts and potentially alters the data.
- **Integrity**: HTTPS ensures that the data sent to and from the server is not tampered with during transmission.

2. Setting Up HTTPS in Flask

To enable HTTPS in your Flask application, you need to:

- Obtain an SSL/TLS certificate from a trusted Certificate Authority (CA).
- Configure Flask to use the certificate for secure communication.

Step 1: Obtain an SSL/TLS Certificate You can either use a certificate issued by a trusted CA or generate a self-signed certificate (although self-signed certificates are not recommended for production environments).

Step 2: Configure Flask for HTTPS Once you have your certificate and key files, you can configure Flask to serve over HTTPS:

python

Copy

```
if __name__ == '__main__':
    app.run(ssl_context=('cert.pem', 'key.pem'))
```

This tells Flask to use the SSL certificate (cert.pem) and the private key (key.pem) when serving requests.

3. Redirect HTTP to HTTPS

To ensure all traffic is encrypted, you should force all HTTP requests to redirect to HTTPS. This can be done by setting up a redirect route for HTTP requests.

python

Copy

```python
from flask import redirect, request


@app.before_request
def redirect_to_https():
    if request.is_secure:
        return
    return redirect(request.url.replace("http://", "https://", 1), code=301)
```

In this example, if the request is made over HTTP, it will be automatically redirected to HTTPS.

4. HSTS (HTTP Strict Transport Security)

HSTS is a security feature that instructs browsers to only connect to the site via HTTPS, even if the user attempts to connect via HTTP. This prevents downgrade attacks, where attackers try to force the client to communicate over an unencrypted connection.

You can enable HSTS by setting the appropriate HTTP header:

python

Copy

```python
@app.after_request
def add_hsts(response):
    response.headers['Strict-Transport-Security'] = 'max-age=31536000; includeSubDomains'
    return response
```

This header tells the browser to only access your site over HTTPS for the next year (max-age=31536000).

5.6 Error Handling and Logging for Security

Effective error handling and logging are essential for identifying potential security vulnerabilities and responding to them promptly. A robust error handling system ensures that users are not exposed to sensitive information in error messages, while logging helps developers monitor and analyze potential security threats.

93

1. Handling Errors Securely

When an error occurs, avoid exposing detailed information about the internal workings of your API, such as stack traces or database errors. This information can be useful to attackers and provide them with insights into your system.

Example:

python

Copy

```
@app.errorhandler(500)
def internal_error(error):
    # Log the error details (excluding sensitive data)
    app.logger.error(f"Server error: {error}")
    return jsonify({'message': 'An unexpected error occurred. Please try again later.'}), 500
```

In this example, when a 500 Internal Server Error occurs, Flask returns a generic error message to the user without revealing sensitive details about the server or database.

2. Logging Security Events

Logging is crucial for identifying unusual activity, failed authentication attempts, and other potential threats. Use Flask's built-in logging module to log critical events, such as failed login attempts, API access patterns, and error responses.

Example of secure logging:

python

Copy

```python
import logging

# Set up logging configuration
logging.basicConfig(level=logging.INFO)
app.logger.setLevel(logging.INFO)


@app.route('/login', methods=['POST'])
def login():
    username = request.json.get('username')
    password = request.json.get('password')
    if username != 'admin' or password != 'secret':
        app.logger.warning(f"Failed login attempt for username: {username}")
        return jsonify({'message': 'Invalid credentials'}), 401
    return jsonify({'message': 'Login successful'})
```

In this example, failed login attempts are logged with a warning message, making it easy to monitor unauthorized access attempts.

3. Protecting Logs

Ensure that your logs do not contain sensitive information such as passwords, API keys, or personal data. You should **sanitize logs** before writing them to prevent accidental leakage of sensitive information.

5.7 Summary & What's Next

In this chapter, we covered important security aspects for ensuring that your Flask API is well-protected from common threats:

- **SQL Injection and XSS Protection**: We discussed how to mitigate risks from SQL injection and XSS by using safe coding practices, input validation, and escaping user data.
- **Using HTTPS**: We highlighted the importance of securing your API with HTTPS and how to configure Flask for HTTPS, including setting up SSL certificates and HSTS.
- **Error Handling and Logging**: We explored how to handle errors securely, ensuring that sensitive information is not exposed in error messages, and discussed logging practices for identifying potential security incidents.

As you continue developing your API, securing it should always be a priority. In the next chapter, we will delve into **API Documentation**—how to document your API effectively, ensuring that it is clear, comprehensive, and accessible to developers.

Chapter 6: API Authentication and Authorization

6.1 Introduction to Authentication and Authorization in Flask APIs

Authentication and authorization are two key concepts that help secure your API and ensure that only legitimate users have access to specific resources.

- **Authentication** is the process of verifying a user's identity. It ensures that the person requesting access to the API is who they claim to be.
- **Authorization** is the process of determining what actions or resources a user can access after their identity has been verified.

When building a Flask API, it's important to implement both authentication and authorization mechanisms to protect sensitive resources and data. In this chapter, we will cover some of the most common approaches to handling authentication and authorization in Flask APIs, including **JSON Web Tokens (JWT)** and **OAuth 2.0**.

Why Authentication and Authorization Matter

- **Protection of Sensitive Data**: Authentication ensures that only authorized users can access sensitive information, such as user data or financial records.
- **Access Control**: Authorization allows you to control what specific users can or cannot do within your API. For instance, an admin might have full access to the API, while regular users can only access their own data.
- **Prevention of Unauthorized Access**: Without proper authentication and authorization, malicious users could potentially bypass restrictions and gain access to resources they shouldn't have access to, leading to security vulnerabilities.

1. Authentication vs. Authorization

- **Authentication** answers the question, "Who are you?"
- **Authorization** answers the question, "What can you do?"

For example:

- A user logs in with their username and password (authentication).
- Once logged in, they are only allowed to access their own profile and not other users' profiles (authorization).

6.2 Implementing JSON Web Tokens (JWT) for Secure Authentication

JSON Web Tokens (JWT) are one of the most popular methods for implementing authentication in modern web APIs. JWT is a compact, self-contained token that is used to verify the identity of the user and securely transmit information between parties. It's often used for stateless authentication, meaning the server doesn't need to store session information.

How JWT Works

- **Sign In**: The user submits their credentials (e.g., username and password) to the API.
- **Token Generation**: If the credentials are valid, the API generates a JWT that contains a payload with user information (e.g., user ID, roles) and a signature to prevent tampering.
- **Token Validation**: For subsequent requests, the client sends the JWT in the authorization header. The server validates the token to ensure that it's valid and not expired, granting access to the protected resources.

1. Structure of a JWT

A JWT consists of three parts:

1. **Header**: Contains metadata about the token, such as the signing algorithm (usually HS256 or RS256).
2. **Payload**: Contains the claims or user data (such as user ID, roles, and token expiration time).
3. **Signature**: A cryptographic signature used to verify that the token was generated by a trusted source and hasn't been tampered with.

A JWT looks like this:

css
Copy
```
header.payload.signature
```

2. Generating a JWT in Flask

To implement JWT authentication in your Flask API, you will need a secret key to sign the token and libraries such as **PyJWT** to generate and decode tokens.

Step 1: Install PyJWT

bash
Copy
```
pip install pyjwt
```

Step 2: Implement JWT Authentication

Here's an example of how to generate and validate JWT tokens in Flask:

99

python

Copy

```python
import jwt
from datetime import datetime, timedelta
from flask import Flask, request, jsonify

app = Flask(__name__)
SECRET_KEY = 'your_secret_key'

# Function to generate JWT token
def generate_jwt(payload):
    expiration = datetime.utcnow() + timedelta(hours=1)
    payload.update({'exp': expiration})
    token = jwt.encode(payload, SECRET_KEY, algorithm='HS256')
    return token

# Route to authenticate user and generate JWT
@app.route('/login', methods=['POST'])
def login():
    data = request.json
    username = data.get('username')
    password = data.get('password')
    if username == 'admin' and password == 'password':  # Simplified authentication
        payload = {'username': username}
        token = generate_jwt(payload)
        return jsonify({'token': token}), 200
    return jsonify({'message': 'Invalid credentials'}), 401

# Protected route that requires JWT for access
@app.route('/protected', methods=['GET'])
```

```
def protected():
    token = request.headers.get('Authorization')
    if not token:
        return jsonify({'message': 'Token is missing'}), 403

    try:
        # Remove "Bearer " prefix from the token
        token = token.split(" ")[1]
        decoded = jwt.decode(token, SECRET_KEY, algorithms=['HS256'])
        return jsonify({'message': f'Welcome {decoded["username"]}'}), 200
    except jwt.ExpiredSignatureError:
        return jsonify({'message': 'Token expired'}), 401
    except jwt.InvalidTokenError:
        return jsonify({'message': 'Invalid token'}), 403

if __name__ == '__main__':
    app.run(debug=True)
```

Explanation:

- The /login route authenticates the user and generates a JWT containing the username. This token is sent back to the client.
- The /protected route requires a valid JWT token in the Authorization header. The token is decoded, and if it's valid, the user is granted access.

3. Verifying and Decoding JWT

When a client sends a JWT in the Authorization header (e.g., Bearer <token>), the server verifies the token's signature using the secret key. If the token is valid and hasn't expired, the user is granted access to the requested resource. If the token is invalid or expired, an error response is returned.

101

4. Best Practices for JWT

- **Set Expiration Times:** Always set an expiration (exp) time for your JWT to limit how long a token is valid.
- **Use HTTPS:** Always transmit JWT tokens over HTTPS to protect them from being intercepted.
- **Store Tokens Securely:** Store JWT tokens in secure HTTP-only cookies or local storage, depending on the needs of your application.

6.3 OAuth 2.0: Integrating with Third-Party Services

OAuth 2.0 is an authorization framework that allows third-party applications to access a user's resources without sharing their credentials. Instead of asking users to provide their username and password, OAuth allows them to log in using their credentials from trusted identity providers like Google, Facebook, or GitHub. OAuth is commonly used for **delegated access** and **third-party authentication**.

How OAuth Works

1. **User Authorization**: The user is redirected to the identity provider (e.g., Google or Facebook) to authorize the third-party application to access their resources.
2. **Access Token**: After the user authorizes the application, the identity provider sends an **access token** to the third-party application. This token allows the application to access the user's data.
3. **Access Protected Resources**: The third-party application uses the access token to make authorized API calls to the service on behalf of the user.

1. Implementing OAuth 2.0 in Flask

To integrate OAuth 2.0 into your Flask API, you can use the **Authlib** library, which simplifies the process of working with OAuth 2.0 providers.

102

Step 1: Install Authlib

bash

Copy

```
pip install Authlib
```

Step 2: OAuth Integration in Flask Here's an example of how to use OAuth 2.0 with Google as the identity provider:

python

Copy

```python
from flask import Flask, redirect, url_for, session
from authlib.integrations.flask_client import OAuth

app = Flask(__name__)
app.secret_key = 'random_secret_key'

oauth = OAuth(app)
google = oauth.register(
    name='google',
    client_id='GOOGLE_CLIENT_ID',
    client_secret='GOOGLE_CLIENT_SECRET',
    authorize_url='https://accounts.google.com/o/oauth2/auth',
    authorize_params=None,
    access_token_url='https://accounts.google.com/o/oauth2/token',
    refresh_token_url=None,
    client_kwargs={'scope': 'openid profile email'},
)

@app.route('/')
```

103

```
def homepage():
    return 'Welcome to the API! Please <a href="/login">login with Google</a>.'

@app.route('/login')
def login():
    redirect_uri = url_for('auth', _external=True)
    return google.authorize_redirect(redirect_uri)

@app.route('/auth')
def auth():
    google.authorize_access_token()
    user = google.parse_id_token()
    session['user'] = user
    return 'You are logged in as ' + user['email']

if __name__ == '__main__':
    app.run(debug=True)
```

Explanation:

- The /login route redirects the user to Google's OAuth 2.0 authorization page.
- After the user logs in, Google redirects back to /auth, where the Flask application retrieves the access token and user information.
- The user data is stored in the session, allowing the application to access user details.

2. Benefits of Using OAuth

- **Delegated Access:** OAuth allows users to grant permission to third-party applications without sharing their credentials.

- **Third-Party Authentication:** OAuth allows users to authenticate via trusted identity providers (e.g., Google, Facebook, etc.), improving user experience and security.
- **Access Control:** OAuth allows you to define fine-grained access control by using **scopes** to specify the resources that can be accessed.

3. OAuth Scopes

OAuth allows you to define **scopes**, which represent the level of access granted to the third-party application. For example, you might allow read-only access to a user's profile but restrict access to their email address or calendar.

Example of scope in Google OAuth:

python
Copy
```
client_kwargs={'scope': 'openid profile email'}
```

This scope grants access to the user's basic profile and email address.

6.4 User Roles and Permissions in Flask APIs

In many applications, different users need different levels of access to resources. For example, an administrator may have full access to all resources, while a regular user can only view their own data. Implementing **user roles** and **permissions** helps manage who can access and modify different resources in your Flask API.

1. Defining User Roles

User roles define the level of access that a user has within the API. Common roles include:

- **Admin**: Full access to all resources and functionalities.
- **User**: Limited access, usually only to their own data or certain non-sensitive resources.
- **Guest**: A very restricted role, often used for read-only access to public resources.

2. Implementing User Roles in Flask

You can implement user roles and permissions in your Flask API by creating a user model with a role field. Here's an example using **Flask-SQLAlchemy** for storing user roles in a database.

Step 1: Define User Model with Roles

python

Copy

```python
from flask import Flask, request, jsonify

from flask_sqlalchemy import SQLAlchemy

from flask_login import UserMixin


app = Flask(__name__)

app.config['SQLALCHEMY_DATABASE_URI'] = 'sqlite:///users.db'

db = SQLAlchemy(app)


class User(db.Model, UserMixin):

    id = db.Column(db.Integer, primary_key=True)
```

```python
username = db.Column(db.String(80), unique=True, nullable=False)

role = db.Column(db.String(50), nullable=False)


# Example roles: Admin, User
```

Step 2: Define Role-based Access Control (RBAC) Using the role defined in the User model, you can restrict access to certain routes based on user roles. Here's how to implement role-based access control (RBAC) to manage permissions:

python

Copy

```python
from flask_login import login_required, current_user


# Decorator to enforce role-based access control
def role_required(role):
    def wrapper(fn):
        @login_required
        def wrapped(*args, **kwargs):
            if current_user.role != role:
                return jsonify({'message': 'Access forbidden'}), 403
            return fn(*args, **kwargs)
```

```
    return wrapped

  return wrapper


# Example routes

@app.route('/admin')

@role_required('Admin')

def admin_dashboard():

    return jsonify({'message': 'Welcome to the Admin Dashboard'})


@app.route('/user')

@role_required('User')

def user_profile():

    return jsonify({'message': f'Welcome, {current_user.username}'})
```

In this example:

- The role_required() decorator checks if the logged-in user has the correct role before allowing access to the route.
- The /admin route is only accessible by users with the Admin role, and the /user route is for users with the User role.

3. Permissions

Permissions specify what actions a user can perform on specific resources. For example:

- **Read**: Viewing data.
- **Write**: Modifying or creating data.
- **Delete**: Deleting data.

You can implement permissions by associating them with roles or assigning them directly to users. One way to handle this is to create a **permissions table** and associate it with users and roles.

6.5 Multi-Factor Authentication in Flask

Multi-Factor Authentication (MFA) is an additional layer of security used to ensure that users are who they say they are. Instead of relying solely on a username and password, MFA requires users to provide a second form of verification, such as a one-time password (OTP) sent via SMS or an authenticator app.

1. Why Use Multi-Factor Authentication?

MFA greatly enhances the security of your API by making it much harder for attackers to gain unauthorized access, even if they have compromised the user's password. Common forms of MFA include:

- **Something you know**: A password or PIN.
- **Something you have**: A physical device, such as a smartphone or a hardware token.
- **Something you are**: Biometric factors like fingerprints or facial recognition.

2. Implementing MFA with Flask

To implement MFA in Flask, you can use libraries like **PyOTP** (for generating time-based OTPs) and **Flask-Security** for user authentication.

Step 1: Install PyOTP

bash

Copy

```
pip install pyotp
```

Step 2: Generate OTP You can generate time-based OTPs (TOTP) using PyOTP. Here's how to set it up:

python

Copy

```
import pyotp

from flask import Flask, request, jsonify


app = Flask(__name__)


# Generate a secret key for the user (store it securely in your database)

def generate_totp_secret():

    return pyotp.random_base32()
```

```python
# Generate the OTP using the secret key

def generate_otp(secret):

    totp = pyotp.TOTP(secret)

    return totp.now()


@app.route('/enable-mfa', methods=['POST'])

def enable_mfa():

    secret = generate_totp_secret()

    return jsonify({'secret': secret}), 200


@app.route('/verify-mfa', methods=['POST'])

def verify_mfa():

    user_otp = request.json.get('otp')

    secret = request.json.get('secret')  # Retrieve secret from DB

    totp = pyotp.TOTP(secret)


    if totp.verify(user_otp):

        return jsonify({'message': 'MFA verified successfully'}), 200
```

111

```
return jsonify({'message': 'Invalid MFA token'}), 401
```

Explanation:

- The /enable-mfa route generates a new TOTP secret for the user and returns it.
- The /verify-mfa route checks the user's OTP against the stored secret.

3. Third-Party MFA Services

For better security and convenience, you can integrate third-party MFA providers such as:

- **Authy**
- **Google Authenticator**
- **Twilio** (for SMS-based OTPs)

By using these services, you can easily add SMS-based or app-based MFA without having to build your own solution.

6.6 API Rate Limiting for Security

API rate limiting is an important security measure that helps prevent abuse and protects your API from being overwhelmed by excessive traffic. By restricting the number of requests a client can make within a given time frame, rate limiting helps to prevent DoS (Denial of Service) attacks, brute force attempts, and resource exhaustion.

1. Why Use Rate Limiting?

- **Protect Resources**: Prevent excessive requests from consuming server resources.

- **Mitigate DDoS Attacks**: Slow down or stop large-scale attacks that target your API.
- **Improve Reliability**: Ensure that legitimate users can access your API by limiting the impact of malicious or abusive traffic.

2. Implementing Rate Limiting in Flask

Flask provides extensions such as **Flask-Limiter** to easily implement rate limiting. Here's an example:

Step 1: Install Flask-Limiter

bash

Copy

```
pip install Flask-Limiter
```

Step 2: Configure Rate Limiting

python

Copy

```
from flask import Flask, jsonify

from flask_limiter import Limiter

from flask_limiter.util import get_remote_address


app = Flask(__name__)

limiter = Limiter(app, key_func=get_remote_address)
```

```
@app.route('/api/resource')

@limiter.limit("5 per minute")

def resource():

    return jsonify({'message': 'This is a rate-limited resource'})


@app.route('/api/another_resource')

@limiter.limit("10 per hour")

def another_resource():

    return jsonify({'message': 'This is another rate-limited resource'})
```

Explanation:

- The @limiter.limit() decorator restricts the number of requests that can be made to the specified endpoint. In this case, the /api/resource endpoint allows only 5 requests per minute from the same IP address, while /api/another_resource allows 10 requests per hour.
- get_remote_address ensures that the rate limit is applied per IP address, but you could adjust this based on the client's API key or session ID if needed.

3. Rate Limiting Strategies

You can implement different rate limiting strategies depending on your use case:

- **Global Rate Limiting**: Limit the number of requests globally across all endpoints.
- **Per-User Rate Limiting**: Limit requests based on the authenticated user.
- **Burst Rate Limiting**: Allow a burst of requests followed by a period of slower requests to account for irregular traffic patterns.

4. Handling Rate Limiting Exceedance

When a client exceeds the rate limit, Flask-Limiter will automatically return a 429 Too Many Requests response. You can customize this behavior and provide more detailed error messages:

python

Copy

```
@app.errorhandler(429)

def ratelimit_error(e):

    return jsonify(error="ratelimit exceeded", message=str(e.description)), 429
```

6.7 Summary & What's Next

In this chapter, we covered various aspects of API security related to authentication and access control:

- **User Roles and Permissions**: We discussed how to define roles and enforce role-based access control (RBAC) in Flask, ensuring that users have appropriate levels of access to resources.

- **Multi-Factor Authentication**: We explored how to implement MFA in Flask to enhance security by requiring multiple forms of verification.
- **API Rate Limiting**: We looked at how to prevent abuse and resource exhaustion by limiting the number of requests a user can make within a specific time frame.

As we move forward, the next chapter will focus on **API Versioning and Documentation**. We'll explore how to version your API to maintain compatibility with existing clients while supporting new features, and how to document your API to ensure it's clear and easy to use for developers.

Chapter 7: Working with Databases in Flask

7.1 Introduction to Database Integration in Flask

Databases are an integral part of modern web applications, enabling them to store and retrieve data efficiently. Flask, being a lightweight framework, doesn't impose any specific database choice. This flexibility means that you can integrate Flask with a variety of databases, both relational (SQL) and non-relational (NoSQL), depending on the needs of your application.

In this chapter, we will explore how to integrate databases into a Flask application, focusing on relational databases (SQL) first and introducing SQLAlchemy, which is Flask's default ORM (Object Relational Mapper) tool. We will also discuss NoSQL databases briefly, to give you a broad view of your options.

1. What is Database Integration in Flask?

Database integration in Flask involves connecting your Flask application to a database system where you can store, query, update, and delete data. This is done by setting up a connection to the database, configuring models (representations of your data), and implementing routes to interact with this data.

Flask can integrate with various database systems, but the most common choices are:

- **Relational Databases (SQL)**: These databases use structured query language (SQL) for defining and managing data. Examples include **PostgreSQL**, **MySQL**, and **SQLite**.
- **Non-relational Databases (NoSQL)**: These databases store data in formats such as documents, key-value pairs, graphs, or wide-column stores. Examples include **MongoDB**, **Redis**, and **Cassandra**.

In this chapter, we'll focus on **relational databases**, which are widely used with Flask for handling structured data with clear relationships.

2. Why Use SQL in Flask?

Relational databases are an excellent choice for applications that require structured data storage, complex queries, and transactional integrity. SQL databases excel in applications that need to ensure data consistency and relationships between different pieces of data. For instance, Flask can easily interact with SQL databases when developing applications like e-commerce platforms, user management systems, or content management systems (CMS).

7.2 Choosing the Right Database: SQL vs. NoSQL

When designing a Flask application, one of the first decisions you'll face is whether to use an SQL or NoSQL database. Both have their strengths, and choosing the right one depends on the nature of your data, the application's requirements, and how you intend to scale.

1. SQL Databases

SQL databases, such as **PostgreSQL**, **MySQL**, and **SQLite**, are based on relational models, which means they store data in tables with rows and columns. Each row in a table represents a record, and each column represents an attribute of that record. SQL databases use structured query language (SQL) for data manipulation.

Advantages of SQL databases:

- **Structured Data**: Ideal for applications where data can be structured into tables with predefined schemas (e.g., user records, orders, inventory).

- **ACID Compliance**: SQL databases are ACID-compliant, which ensures atomicity, consistency, isolation, and durability for transactions. This makes them suitable for applications that require data integrity, such as banking systems or e-commerce platforms.
- **Join Queries**: SQL databases allow for complex queries that can join multiple tables together, making it easy to retrieve data from different related tables.

When to use SQL:

- Your data has clear relationships (e.g., one-to-many, many-to-many).
- You need to perform complex queries and joins.
- You require ACID-compliant transactions (e.g., handling financial data).

2. NoSQL Databases

NoSQL databases, such as **MongoDB**, **Cassandra**, and **Redis**, are designed for applications that require flexible, scalable data storage. Unlike SQL databases, NoSQL databases don't require a fixed schema and can handle unstructured or semi-structured data (e.g., JSON documents, key-value pairs).

Advantages of NoSQL databases:

- **Flexible Schema**: NoSQL databases allow you to store data in a flexible format, which is ideal for applications where the data schema may change over time.
- **Scalability**: Many NoSQL databases are designed to scale horizontally, making them suitable for applications that expect high traffic or large volumes of unstructured data (e.g., social media, sensor data).
- **High Availability and Performance**: NoSQL databases often offer better performance and availability in distributed systems, making them well-suited for applications with large datasets or real-time data processing.

When to use NoSQL:

- Your data is unstructured or semi-structured (e.g., documents, key-value pairs).
- You need high scalability and flexible schema design.
- You want fast writes and don't need complex joins or transactions.

3. Choosing Between SQL and NoSQL

- **SQL**: If your data is structured and you need ACID compliance and relational integrity (e.g., e-commerce, banking), SQL is a good choice.
- **NoSQL**: If your application requires fast scalability, flexible schema, and can tolerate eventual consistency (e.g., big data, social networks), NoSQL might be the better option.

7.3 Using SQLAlchemy to Integrate with Relational Databases

SQLAlchemy is the default Object Relational Mapper (ORM) used in Flask applications to interact with SQL databases. It provides a Pythonic way to define models and interact with the database without writing raw SQL queries. SQLAlchemy allows you to map Python classes to database tables and perform CRUD (Create, Read, Update, Delete) operations.

1. Installing SQLAlchemy

To integrate SQLAlchemy with Flask, you need to install both **Flask-SQLAlchemy** and **SQLAlchemy**:

bash

Copy

```
pip install Flask-SQLAlchemy
```

2. Setting Up SQLAlchemy in Flask

Once you've installed Flask-SQLAlchemy, you can set up the database connection in your Flask application:

Example Setup:

python
Copy

```python
from flask import Flask
from flask_sqlalchemy import SQLAlchemy

app = Flask(__name__)
app.config['SQLALCHEMY_DATABASE_URI'] = 'sqlite:///mydatabase.db'  # Use SQLite for this example
app.config['SQLALCHEMY_TRACK_MODIFICATIONS'] = False  # Disable modification tracking for performance

db = SQLAlchemy(app)  # Initialize the SQLAlchemy object
```

In this example, we are using SQLite as our database, but you can replace 'sqlite:///mydatabase.db' with a URI for other databases like MySQL or PostgreSQL (e.g., 'postgresql://user:password@localhost/mydatabase').

3. Defining Models

In SQLAlchemy, models are Python classes that map to database tables. Here's how to define a simple User model:

python
Copy

```python
class User(db.Model):
```

121

```python
id = db.Column(db.Integer, primary_key=True)
username = db.Column(db.String(80), unique=True, nullable=False)
email = db.Column(db.String(120), unique=True, nullable=False)

def __repr__(self):
    return f'<User {self.username}>'
```

In this example:

- id, username, and email are columns in the User table.
- db.Column() defines the type of the column, and we specify properties such as primary_key=True, nullable=False, and unique=True.
- The __repr__ method provides a string representation of the User object.

4. Creating and Manipulating Data

Once you've defined your models, you can interact with the database using SQLAlchemy's ORM capabilities. For example, you can create, query, update, and delete records:

Creating a new user:

python
Copy
```python
@app.route('/add_user', methods=['POST'])
def add_user():
    user = User(username='john_doe', email='john@example.com')
    db.session.add(user)
    db.session.commit()
    return f'User {user.username} added!'
```

Querying users:

python
Copy
```python
@app.route('/users')
def get_users():
    users = User.query.all()  # Retrieve all users
    return {'users': [user.username for user in users]}
```

Updating a user:

python
Copy
```python
@app.route('/update_user/<int:user_id>', methods=['PUT'])
def update_user(user_id):
    user = User.query.get(user_id)
    if user:
        user.username = 'new_username'
        db.session.commit()
        return f'User {user_id} updated!'
    return 'User not found', 404
```

Deleting a user:

python
Copy
```python
@app.route('/delete_user/<int:user_id>', methods=['DELETE'])
def delete_user(user_id):
    user = User.query.get(user_id)
    if user:
```

123

```
        db.session.delete(user)
        db.session.commit()
        return f'User {user_id} deleted!'
    return 'User not found', 404
```

5. Handling Relationships Between Models

SQLAlchemy supports defining relationships between tables (models) through **foreign keys** and **relationships**. For example, a Post can be related to a User, where each post is created by a specific user.

Example of a one-to-many relationship:

python
Copy
```
class Post(db.Model):
    id = db.Column(db.Integer, primary_key=True)
    title = db.Column(db.String(100), nullable=False)
    content = db.Column(db.Text, nullable=False)
    user_id = db.Column(db.Integer, db.ForeignKey('user.id'), nullable=False)
    user = db.relationship('User', back_populates='posts')

User.posts = db.relationship('Post', back_populates='user')
```

In this example:

- Post has a foreign key user_id that references the User model.
- The user relationship is used to access the user associated with a post, and the posts relationship allows access to the posts associated with a user.

124

6. Migrations with Flask-Migrate

As your application grows, you'll likely need to make changes to your database schema. To manage these changes, Flask-Migrate is an extension that integrates with Alembic, a database migration tool.

Step 1: Install Flask-Migrate

bash
Copy

```
pip install Flask-Migrate
```

Step 2: Set Up Migrations

python
Copy

```
from flask_migrate import Migrate

migrate = Migrate(app, db)
```

Step 3: Create and Apply Migrations

bash
Copy

```
flask db init        # Initialize migration repository
flask db migrate     # Generate migration script
flask db upgrade     # Apply the migration to the database
```

7.4 Working with MongoDB and Flask for NoSQL Applications

While SQL databases are great for structured data with well-defined relationships, **NoSQL databases**, like **MongoDB**, are often better suited for unstructured or semi-structured data. MongoDB, a document-based NoSQL database, stores data in JSON-like format (BSON), allowing for more flexibility in schema design. This is especially useful for applications that need to store diverse types of data, and scale horizontally.

1. Setting Up MongoDB with Flask

To integrate MongoDB with Flask, you can use the **PyMongo** extension, which provides a simple interface for interacting with MongoDB from Flask.

Step 1: Install PyMongo

bash
Copy
```
pip install Flask-PyMongo
```

Step 2: Configure Flask to Connect to MongoDB Here's how to set up MongoDB in your Flask application:

python
Copy
```
from flask import Flask, jsonify
from flask_pymongo import PyMongo

app = Flask(__name__)
```

```python
# Configure MongoDB URI
app.config["MONGO_URI"] = "mongodb://localhost:27017/mydatabase"
mongo = PyMongo(app)

@app.route('/add_user', methods=['POST'])
def add_user():
    user = {'username': 'john_doe', 'email': 'john@example.com'}
    mongo.db.users.insert_one(user)
    return jsonify({'message': 'User added successfully'}), 200
```

Explanation:

- The MONGO_URI configuration specifies the MongoDB connection string. You can replace the URI with your MongoDB server details.
- The mongo.db.users.insert_one(user) inserts a new document into the users collection.

2. Querying Data in MongoDB

MongoDB allows you to perform complex queries using **filters** and **projections**. Here's how to query data in Flask using MongoDB:

Step 1: Retrieve a Single Document

python
Copy

```python
@app.route('/get_user/<username>', methods=['GET'])
def get_user(username):
    user = mongo.db.users.find_one({'username': username})
    if user:
        return jsonify({'username': user['username'], 'email': user['email']}), 200
```

127

```
    return jsonify({'message': 'User not found'}), 404
```

Step 2: Retrieve Multiple Documents

python

Copy

```
@app.route('/get_all_users', methods=['GET'])
def get_all_users():
    users = mongo.db.users.find()
    users_list = [{'username': user['username'], 'email': user['email']} for user in users]
    return jsonify(users_list), 200
```

Explanation:

- find_one() **retrieves a single document based on a filter** (e.g., {'username': 'john_doe'}).
- find() **retrieves all documents in the collection. You can also add filters to limit the results** (e.g., find({'status': 'active'})).

3. Benefits of Using MongoDB in Flask

- **Flexible Schema**: MongoDB allows you to store documents without a fixed schema, making it easier to adapt to changing requirements.
- **Horizontal Scalability**: MongoDB is designed for scaling out, making it ideal for handling large datasets and high traffic.
- **Fast Writes**: MongoDB provides high throughput for write-heavy applications, which is particularly useful in real-time applications.

7.5 Query Optimization for Flask APIs

As your Flask application grows and handles more data, it's essential to optimize your database queries for performance. Slow queries can negatively affect the user experience and overall application performance. Here are some strategies to optimize queries in Flask APIs, both for SQL and NoSQL databases.

1. Indexing

Indexing is one of the most effective ways to improve the speed of database queries. Indexes help the database locate data without scanning the entire table or collection.

- **SQL Indexing**: In SQLAlchemy, you can add indexes to columns that are frequently queried.

Example:

python
Copy

```python
class User(db.Model):
    id = db.Column(db.Integer, primary_key=True)
    username = db.Column(db.String(80), unique=True, index=True)  # Index on username
```

- **MongoDB Indexing**: In MongoDB, you can create indexes on fields that are frequently queried.

Example:

python
Copy

```python
mongo.db.users.create_index([('username', pymongo.ASCENDING)])
```

129

2. Query Limiting

Limiting the number of results returned by a query can help reduce the load on the database and improve response times. Both SQL and MongoDB support query limiting.

- **SQL Limiting**:

python
Copy
```
users = User.query.limit(10).all()  # Retrieve only the first 10 users
```

- **MongoDB Limiting**:

python
Copy
```
users = mongo.db.users.find().limit(10)
```

3. Avoiding N+1 Query Problem

The N+1 query problem occurs when a query retrieves a large set of rows and then performs additional queries for each row. This can significantly degrade performance.

- **SQL Optimization**: Use **eager loading** to load related objects in a single query.

Example (SQLAlchemy):

python
Copy
```
from sqlalchemy.orm import joinedload

users = User.query.options(joinedload(User.posts)).all()
```
130

- **MongoDB Optimization**: Use **$lookup** to perform joins between collections instead of querying for each document individually.

4. Query Caching

For frequently accessed data, consider using caching techniques such as **Redis** to cache query results. This reduces the need to query the database for the same data multiple times.

Example (Flask-Caching with Redis):

python
Copy

```python
from flask_caching import Cache
cache = Cache(app, config={'CACHE_TYPE': 'redis'})

@app.route('/get_user/<username>', methods=['GET'])
@cache.cached(timeout=60)
def get_user(username):
    user = mongo.db.users.find_one({'username': username})
    if user:
        return jsonify({'username': user['username'], 'email': user['email']}), 200
    return jsonify({'message': 'User not found'}), 404
```

5. Profiling Queries

Profiling allows you to track how long each query takes, helping you identify slow queries that need optimization. Both SQLAlchemy and MongoDB provide ways to profile queries.

- **SQLAlchemy**: Use session.execute() and explain() for query profiling.
- **MongoDB**: Use explain() to get detailed query execution plans.

Example (MongoDB):

python
Copy
```
query = mongo.db.users.find({'status': 'active'})
explanation = query.explain()
print(explanation)
```

6. Denormalization (NoSQL)

In NoSQL databases like MongoDB, you may opt for **denormalization**, where you store duplicate data to reduce the number of queries needed for complex joins. This approach improves read performance at the cost of data duplication.

7.6 Database Migrations in Flask with Flask-Migrate

As your application evolves, you will need to make changes to your database schema, such as adding new tables, modifying existing ones, or renaming columns. **Database migrations** handle these schema changes in a consistent way, ensuring that the database schema is always in sync with the application code.

1. Setting Up Flask-Migrate

Flask-Migrate is an extension that integrates **Alembic**, a database migration tool, with Flask and SQLAlchemy. It allows you to track database schema changes and apply them incrementally.

Step 1: Install Flask-Migrate

bash

Copy

```bash
pip install Flask-Migrate
```

Step 2: Set Up Flask-Migrate

python

Copy

```python
from flask_migrate import Migrate

migrate = Migrate(app, db)
```

Step 3: Initialize Migration Repository

bash

Copy

```bash
flask db init  # Create migration directory
```

2. Creating Migrations

After making changes to your models, you can generate migration scripts with the following command:

bash

Copy

```bash
flask db migrate -m "Added new column to User model"
```

Flask-Migrate compares the current state of the database with the models in your code and generates a migration script to apply the changes.

3. Applying Migrations

To apply the generated migrations to the database, use:

bash

Copy

```
flask db upgrade
```

This will apply the migration and update the database schema.

4. Downgrading Migrations

If you need to revert a migration, use:

bash

Copy

```
flask db downgrade
```

This command will undo the most recent migration, allowing you to roll back changes.

7.7 Summary & What's Next

In this chapter, we explored various aspects of database integration in Flask:

- **Database Integration**: We discussed how to integrate both SQL and NoSQL databases into your Flask application. We focused on MongoDB for NoSQL applications and SQLAlchemy for relational databases.

- **Query Optimization**: We covered strategies for optimizing database queries, including indexing, limiting results, avoiding the N+1 query problem, and using caching to improve performance.
- **Database Migrations**: We learned how to use **Flask-Migrate** to manage schema changes and migrations in your Flask application.

In the next chapter, we will explore **API Versioning and Documentation**, covering best practices for versioning your API and documenting it effectively to ensure that it is both maintainable and user-friendly for developers.

Chapter 8: Building Advanced API Features

8.1 Implementing File Uploads and Downloads

File uploads and downloads are common features in modern APIs, allowing users to interact with binary data, such as images, PDFs, or documents. Flask makes it easy to handle file uploads and downloads with its built-in tools. In this section, we'll go over how to implement both file uploads (allowing users to send files to the server) and file downloads (allowing users to retrieve files from the server).

1. Handling File Uploads in Flask

Flask provides a simple way to handle file uploads via the request.files object. To upload files, you typically need a POST route that handles file input from a form or API client.

Step 1: Setting Up the File Upload Form To allow file uploads, you first need to create an HTML form with an enctype="multipart/form-data" attribute. This form will allow users to send binary data.

Example:

html

Copy

```html
<form action="/upload" method="POST" enctype="multipart/form-data">
    <input type="file" name="file">
    <button type="submit">Upload File</button>
</form>
```

Step 2: Handling File Uploads in Flask In Flask, you can access the uploaded file using request.files['file']. You can then save the file to the server or process it as needed.

136

Example of handling file uploads:

python

Copy

```python
from flask import Flask, request, jsonify
import os

app = Flask(__name__)

# Configure the folder for storing uploaded files
app.config['UPLOAD_FOLDER'] = './uploads'
app.config['ALLOWED_EXTENSIONS'] = {'png', 'jpg', 'jpeg', 'gif'}

# Check if the file extension is allowed
def allowed_file(filename):
    return '.' in filename and filename.rsplit('.', 1)[1].lower() in app.config['ALLOWED_EXTENSIONS']

@app.route('/upload', methods=['POST'])
def upload_file():
    if 'file' not in request.files:
        return jsonify({'message': 'No file part'}), 400

    file = request.files['file']

    if file.filename == '':
        return jsonify({'message': 'No selected file'}), 400

    if file and allowed_file(file.filename):
        filename = os.path.join(app.config['UPLOAD_FOLDER'], file.filename)
```

```
file.save(filename)
    return jsonify({'message': 'File uploaded successfully', 'file_path': filename}), 200
else:
    return jsonify({'message': 'File type not allowed'}), 400
```

Explanation:

- The file is accessed from request.files['file'].
- The file is saved to a directory specified by UPLOAD_FOLDER.
- The file extension is validated using allowed_file() to ensure only specific types of files (like images) are uploaded.

2. Handling File Downloads in Flask

File downloads allow users to retrieve files stored on the server. Flask's send_from_directory() function simplifies the process of serving files for download.

Example of handling file downloads:

python

Copy

```
from flask import send_from_directory

@app.route('/download/<filename>', methods=['GET'])
def download_file(filename):
    return send_from_directory(app.config['UPLOAD_FOLDER'], filename)
```

Explanation:

- The send_from_directory() function sends a file from a specific directory (in this case, UPLOAD_FOLDER) to the client.

138

- The filename is passed as part of the URL, and Flask retrieves the file from the server and sends it back to the client for download.

3. Security Considerations for File Uploads

When implementing file uploads and downloads, security is a top concern. Here are some best practices:

- **Limit File Types**: Only allow certain file extensions to prevent malicious files from being uploaded.
- **Check File Size**: Set limits on the file size to prevent overloading the server.
- **Sanitize Filenames**: Ensure that filenames are sanitized to avoid issues like directory traversal or overwriting sensitive files.
- **Store Files Securely**: Store uploaded files in a secure location with appropriate access controls.

8.2 Working with External APIs and Services

Often, you may need to integrate your Flask API with external services, such as third-party APIs, cloud storage, or external databases. Flask makes it simple to communicate with these services via **HTTP requests**, typically using libraries like **Requests**.

1. Making HTTP Requests in Flask

Flask doesn't provide built-in support for making HTTP requests, but you can use the popular **Requests** library to interact with external APIs.

Step 1: Install Requests

bash

Copy

139

```
pip install requests
```

Step 2: Making GET and POST Requests to External APIs

Here's how you can use **Requests** to make GET and POST requests to external APIs:

GET Request Example:

python

Copy

```python
import requests

@app.route('/get_data', methods=['GET'])
def get_data():
    response = requests.get('https://api.example.com/data')
    if response.status_code == 200:
        return jsonify(response.json()), 200
    else:
        return jsonify({'message': 'Failed to retrieve data'}), 400
```

POST Request Example:

python

Copy

```python
@app.route('/send_data', methods=['POST'])
def send_data():
    data = {'username': 'john_doe', 'email': 'john@example.com'}
    response = requests.post('https://api.example.com/submit', json=data)
    if response.status_code == 201:
        return jsonify({'message': 'Data sent successfully'}), 201
```

```
else:
    return jsonify({'message': 'Failed to send data'}), 400
```

Explanation:

- requests.get() sends a GET request to an external API and retrieves the response.
- requests.post() sends a POST request to an external API, passing data in JSON format.

2. Handling Authentication with External APIs

Many external APIs require authentication, such as an **API key** or **OAuth token**, to ensure that only authorized users can access the service. Flask makes it easy to handle these authentication methods.

Example: Using an API Key in a Header

python
Copy

```python
@app.route('/get_protected_data', methods=['GET'])
def get_protected_data():
    headers = {'Authorization': 'Bearer YOUR_API_KEY'}
    response = requests.get('https://api.example.com/protected_data', headers=headers)
    if response.status_code == 200:
        return jsonify(response.json()), 200
    else:
        return jsonify({'message': 'Unauthorized or failed request'}), 401
```

Explanation:

- The API key is sent in the Authorization header using the Bearer scheme. The external service uses this key to authenticate the request.

3. Error Handling in External API Integration

When integrating with external services, you need to account for potential errors, such as:

- **Network issues**
- **API service downtime**
- **Invalid responses**

You can handle errors gracefully using try-except blocks:

python

Copy

```python
try:
    response = requests.get('https://api.example.com/data')
    response.raise_for_status()  # Raise an error for bad status codes
except requests.exceptions.RequestException as e:
    return jsonify({'message': f'Error occurred: {str(e)}'}), 500
```

This approach helps ensure your Flask application can recover from errors and provide helpful messages to the user.

8.3 Handling Background Tasks with Celery in Flask

Certain tasks in a web application, such as sending emails, processing images, or interacting with slow external APIs, can take a significant amount of time. Performing

142

these tasks synchronously (i.e., blocking the main request-response cycle) can negatively impact the user experience. To solve this, we can use **Celery**, a distributed task queue, to handle long-running tasks in the background.

1. Setting Up Celery with Flask

Step 1: Install Celery and Redis To get started with Celery in Flask, you'll need to install Celery and a message broker, like Redis, to manage background tasks.

bash

Copy

```
pip install Celery redis
```

Step 2: Configure Celery in Flask In this example, we will use **Redis** as the broker for Celery. You'll also need to configure Celery within your Flask application.

python

Copy

```
from flask import Flask, jsonify
from celery import Celery

app = Flask(__name__)

# Configure Celery to use Redis as the broker
app.config['CELERY_BROKER_URL'] = 'redis://localhost:6379/0'
app.config['CELERY_RESULT_BACKEND'] = 'redis://localhost:6379/0'
celery = Celery(app.name, broker=app.config['CELERY_BROKER_URL'])
celery.conf.update(app.config)
```

Step 3: Define a Background Task Here's an example of a simple background task that sends an email. You could use Celery to send emails asynchronously, allowing the API to respond quickly to the user without waiting for the email to be sent.

python

Copy

```python
@celery.task
def send_email(user_email):
    # Simulate email sending
    print(f'Sending email to {user_email}')
    return f'Email sent to {user_email}'
```

Step 4: Trigger the Background Task from a Flask Route You can trigger the background task by calling apply_async().

python

Copy

```python
@app.route('/send_email/<user_email>', methods=['POST'])
def send_email_route(user_email):
    send_email.apply_async(args=[user_email])
    return jsonify({'message': 'Email is being sent in the background'}), 200
```

2. Running Celery Worker

To execute the background task, you need to run a Celery worker in a separate process. Open a terminal and run the following command:

bash

Copy

```bash
celery -A app.celery worker
```

144

This starts the Celery worker, which listens for tasks and processes them asynchronously.

3. Benefits of Using Celery

- **Non-blocking**: Long-running tasks are processed in the background, so the main application remains responsive.
- **Distributed**: Celery can be scaled horizontally by adding more worker nodes.
- **Retry Logic**: Celery supports retrying tasks if they fail, ensuring reliable background processing.

8.4 API Rate Limiting and Throttling Techniques

Rate limiting and throttling are essential techniques for ensuring that your API is secure, efficient, and resilient under high traffic. They prevent abuse, protect server resources, and ensure that users can access the API without experiencing delays due to excessive usage.

1. Rate Limiting

Rate limiting restricts the number of API requests a client can make in a specified time frame (e.g., 100 requests per hour). This is crucial for preventing abuse, especially in public APIs, where users may send too many requests, overwhelming the server.

Flask-Limiter is an extension for Flask that makes implementing rate limiting easy. Here's how you can set it up:

Step 1: Install Flask-Limiter

bash

Copy

pip install Flask-Limiter

Step 2: Implement Rate Limiting in Flask You can configure different rate limits for different endpoints using decorators.

python

Copy

```python
from flask import Flask
from flask_limiter import Limiter
from flask_limiter.util import get_remote_address

app = Flask(__name__)
limiter = Limiter(app, key_func=get_remote_address)

@app.route('/resource')
@limiter.limit("5 per minute")  # Limit 5 requests per minute
def resource():
    return "This is a rate-limited resource"

if __name__ == '__main__':
    app.run(debug=True)
```

In this example, the /resource endpoint is limited to 5 requests per minute per client IP. If a client exceeds this limit, they will receive a 429 Too Many Requests error.

2. Throttling

Throttling is a more flexible approach that gradually slows down requests from clients who are overusing the API rather than completely blocking them. This can be useful for

146

APIs where you want to give users a chance to continue interacting with your service, albeit at a slower rate.

You can implement throttling in Flask using the same **Flask-Limiter** extension, by adjusting the rate limits dynamically or applying more restrictive limits as users continue to make requests.

3. Advanced Rate Limiting Strategies

- **Global Rate Limiting**: Apply rate limits across all endpoints, regardless of which route is being accessed.
- **User-specific Rate Limiting**: Apply different limits to different users, based on their roles, authentication status, or subscription plans.
- **Burst Rate Limiting**: Allow for short bursts of traffic before applying more restrictive limits.

Example of user-specific rate limiting:

python

Copy

```
@app.route('/premium_resource')
@limiter.limit("10 per minute", exempt_when=lambda: not
current_user.is_authenticated)
def premium_resource():
    return "This resource is rate-limited for authenticated users"
```

4. Handling Rate Limiting Responses

When a client exceeds the rate limit, it's important to provide clear feedback about the restriction. You can customize the 429 response to give users more context:

python

147

Copy

```
@app.errorhandler(429)
def ratelimit_error(e):
    return jsonify(error="ratelimit exceeded", message="You have exceeded the rate
limit. Please try again later."), 429
```

5. Benefits of Rate Limiting and Throttling

- **Prevents Abuse**: Protects your API from being overwhelmed by too many requests.
- **Enhances Reliability**: Ensures fair access to the API for all users, especially when resources are limited.
- **Improves User Experience**: Rate limiting ensures that users don't experience slowdowns due to excessive traffic.

8.5 Handling CORS (Cross-Origin Resource Sharing)

CORS is a security feature implemented by browsers that prevents websites from making requests to domains other than their own. While CORS helps secure the browser from cross-site scripting attacks, it can sometimes block legitimate API requests from different origins (e.g., if your API is hosted on a different domain from your front-end application).

To allow cross-origin requests in Flask, you need to configure CORS for your API.

1. Why CORS Matters

- **Enables Cross-Origin Requests**: For modern web applications, it's common for APIs and front-end apps to be hosted on different domains (or subdomains). CORS allows these cross-origin requests to go through safely.

- **Security**: CORS also helps prevent malicious websites from making unauthorized requests to your API by controlling which domains are allowed to access your API.

2. Configuring CORS in Flask

You can enable CORS in your Flask application using the **Flask-CORS** extension, which provides an easy way to configure and manage CORS headers.

Step 1: Install Flask-CORS

bash
Copy

```
pip install flask-cors
```

Step 2: Enable CORS in Flask By default, Flask does not include CORS headers in responses. You can add them using Flask-CORS:

python
Copy

```
from flask import Flask, jsonify
from flask_cors import CORS

app = Flask(__name__)

# Enable CORS for all routes
CORS(app)

@app.route('/resource', methods=['GET'])
def resource():
    return jsonify({"message": "This resource is CORS-enabled!"})
```

```
if __name__ == '__main__':
    app.run(debug=True)
```

Step 3: Customize CORS Configuration You can specify which domains are allowed to access your API by configuring the origins parameter in CORS():

python

Copy

```
CORS(app, origins=["https://example.com"])
```

In this example, only requests coming from https://example.com are allowed to access the API.

3. Handling Preflight Requests

Browsers send a preflight OPTIONS request to check whether a cross-origin request is safe. Flask-CORS automatically handles these requests by adding the appropriate headers.

4. Best Practices for CORS

- **Restrict Allowed Origins**: Only allow trusted domains to access your API to prevent unauthorized access.
- **Allow Specific HTTP Methods**: Specify which HTTP methods (e.g., GET, POST) are allowed in cross-origin requests.

python

Copy

```
CORS(app, methods=["GET", "POST"])
```

8.6 Integrating with Real-Time WebSockets in Flask

Real-time communication is an essential feature for applications like chat apps, live notifications, or collaborative tools. One way to achieve real-time communication is through **WebSockets**, which allow for two-way communication between the client and server over a persistent connection.

Flask can integrate with WebSockets using the **Flask-SocketIO** extension.

1. What are WebSockets?

WebSockets provide a full-duplex communication channel that allows the server to push updates to the client as soon as they are available. Unlike traditional HTTP requests, where the client must periodically poll the server, WebSockets enable instant data transfer between the server and the client.

2. Setting Up Flask-SocketIO

Step 1: Install Flask-SocketIO

bash
Copy
```
pip install flask-socketio
```

Step 2: Configure Flask-SocketIO

python
Copy
```
from flask import Flask, render_template
from flask_socketio import SocketIO
```

```python
app = Flask(__name__)
socketio = SocketIO(app)
@app.route('/')
def index():
    return render_template('index.html')
if __name__ == '__main__':
    socketio.run(app)
```

Step 3: Setting Up Client-Side WebSocket To use WebSockets, you'll need to set up a client-side connection. Flask-SocketIO integrates well with JavaScript.

HTML Example:

html

Copy

```html
<script src="https://cdnjs.cloudflare.com/ajax/libs/socket.io/4.0.0/socket.io.js"></script>
<script>
    var socket = io.connect('http://' + document.domain + ':' + location.port);
    socket.on('connect', function() {
        console.log("Connected to WebSocket server");
        socket.emit('message', {data: 'Hello Server!'});
    });
</script>
```

3. Handling Events with Flask-SocketIO

You can listen for events from the client and emit events back to the client.

Server-side example:

python

Copy

```python
from flask_socketio import SocketIO, emit
```

```
@socketio.on('message')
def handle_message(data):
    print('Received message:', data)
    emit('response', {'data': 'Hello Client!'})
```

In this example:

- When the client sends a message event, the server responds by emitting a response event.

4. Benefits of WebSockets in Flask

- **Real-time Communication**: Enables fast, two-way communication between the server and the client, ideal for chat apps, notifications, or live data feeds.
- **Persistent Connections**: WebSockets keep the connection open, so you don't need to repeatedly send requests.
- **Low Latency**: Since WebSockets don't require HTTP overhead, they are suitable for applications that need low-latency data transfer.

5. Scaling WebSockets

Flask-SocketIO can be scaled by using a message broker (like **Redis**) to share WebSocket messages between multiple instances of your Flask application. This allows you to handle large-scale real-time communication.

8.7 Summary & What's Next

In this chapter, we covered a variety of advanced features for building powerful and responsive APIs:

153

- **API Rate Limiting and Throttling**: We discussed how to implement rate limiting and throttling techniques to protect your API from abuse and ensure fair usage.
- **Handling CORS**: We showed how to handle cross-origin requests with **Flask-CORS** and ensure that your API is accessible from different origins securely.
- **Integrating with Real-Time WebSockets**: We introduced **Flask-SocketIO** for real-time communication, enabling your API to handle WebSocket connections for interactive, live applications.

In the next chapter, we will explore **API Versioning and Documentation**, focusing on best practices for versioning your API to ensure that it remains backward-compatible and well-documented for users and developers.

Chapter 9: Testing and Debugging Flask APIs

9.1 Why Testing is Crucial for Flask APIs

Testing is an essential part of software development, especially when it comes to building APIs. For Flask applications, testing ensures that your API behaves as expected, remains secure, and continues to work after changes are made. Testing helps catch bugs early, improves code quality, and provides documentation for the expected behavior of the application. Without proper testing, your Flask API could face reliability issues, security vulnerabilities, and unexpected failures in production.

1. Benefits of Testing Flask APIs

- **Reliability**: Automated tests help ensure that the code continues to work as expected across different environments and after changes are made.
- **Bug Detection**: Testing allows you to catch bugs early before they affect users or the functionality of the API.
- **Code Confidence**: A robust suite of tests increases confidence in the stability and functionality of your API, especially when deploying new features or fixing bugs.
- **Improved Maintenance**: Well-written tests make it easier to maintain and refactor code since you can quickly verify that the changes don't break existing functionality.

2. Types of Tests for Flask APIs

- **Unit Tests**: Focus on testing individual components of the API in isolation, ensuring that each function behaves correctly.

- **Integration Tests**: Test the interactions between different components, such as the database and external services, ensuring that everything works together as expected.
- **Functional Tests**: Test the behavior of the API as a whole, including verifying that each endpoint works as expected under various scenarios.
- **End-to-End Tests**: Simulate real user interactions with the API to test the system as a whole, including routing, authentication, and response handling.

3. Testing is an Ongoing Process

It's important to regularly test your Flask API throughout the development lifecycle. Testing should be integrated into the development process, including continuous integration (CI) systems, where tests are run automatically every time changes are pushed.

9.2 Unit Testing Flask APIs with Pytest

Unit testing involves testing individual units of code (e.g., functions, methods, or classes) in isolation to verify their correctness. In Flask, unit tests often involve testing routes, views, or business logic.

1. Setting Up Pytest for Flask

Pytest is a popular testing framework for Python that makes it easy to write simple as well as complex test cases. To begin unit testing with Pytest in Flask, you need to install it:

bash
Copy
```
pip install pytest
```

2. Writing Unit Tests for Flask APIs

In Flask, you can use Flask's built-in test client to simulate requests to your API and verify the responses.

Example of testing a simple route:

python
Copy
```python
import pytest
from flask import Flask, jsonify

# Create a simple Flask app
app = Flask(__name__)

@app.route('/hello')
def hello():
    return jsonify(message="Hello, World!")

# Unit test for the /hello route
def test_hello():
    with app.test_client() as client:
        response = client.get('/hello')
        data = response.get_json()

        assert response.status_code == 200
        assert data['message'] == "Hello, World!"
```

Explanation:

- app.test_client() creates a test client that can send requests to the Flask app.

- client.get('/hello') simulates a GET request to the /hello route.
- response.get_json() retrieves the JSON response from the API.
- The assert statements check if the response status is 200 OK and if the message returned is "Hello, World!".

3. Testing API with Different Methods (GET, POST, etc.)

You can use different HTTP methods (GET, POST, PUT, DELETE, etc.) to test various endpoints.

Example: Testing POST request

python
Copy

```
@app.route('/create', methods=['POST'])
def create_item():
    data = request.get_json()
    return jsonify(item=data['name']), 201


def test_create_item():
    with app.test_client() as client:
        response = client.post('/create', json={'name': 'item1'})
        data = response.get_json()

        assert response.status_code == 201
        assert data['item'] == 'item1'
```

In this example, we test a POST route /create that expects a JSON payload. We send a POST request with JSON data and assert that the returned item matches the input data.

4. Running Tests with Pytest

Once you've written your unit tests, you can run them using Pytest. From the terminal, simply run:

bash

Copy

```
pytest
```

Pytest will discover and run all the test cases defined in your Flask app.

5. Testing Database Interactions

For unit testing with Flask and databases, you can use a **test database** (typically in-memory or temporary) that mimics the production database. This ensures that tests don't modify real data.

Example (using SQLAlchemy):

python

Copy

```python
from flask_sqlalchemy import SQLAlchemy

db = SQLAlchemy(app)

# Create a test model
class User(db.Model):
    id = db.Column(db.Integer, primary_key=True)
    username = db.Column(db.String(80))

# Test function
def test_create_user():
```

159

```python
with app.app_context():
    db.create_all()
    user = User(username="testuser")
    db.session.add(user)
    db.session.commit()

    saved_user = User.query.first()
    assert saved_user.username == "testuser"
```

In this example, we create a test database model, perform operations like adding a user, and verify that the data is stored correctly.

9.3 Integration Testing and Mocking Dependencies

Integration testing is used to test how different components of the application work together. This type of testing is crucial to ensure that your database, external services, and API logic work as expected when combined.

1. Integration Testing in Flask

Integration tests in Flask often involve interacting with the actual database, external APIs, or third-party services. The goal is to test the flow of data and ensure that multiple components work together.

Example:

python
Copy
```python
def test_integration():
    with app.test_client() as client:
```

```python
response = client.get('/users')
assert response.status_code == 200
assert len(response.get_json()) > 0  # Assuming there are users in the DB
```

In this case, we are testing an endpoint that fetches a list of users from the database. This test ensures that the API returns the correct data and interacts with the database correctly.

2. Mocking External Dependencies

When testing APIs that interact with external services (like APIs, databases, or file systems), it's often impractical to rely on real services during tests. **Mocking** allows you to simulate the behavior of these external dependencies.

Step 1: Using unittest.mock for Mocking The unittest.mock module allows you to replace real objects with mock objects that simulate their behavior.

Example of Mocking an External API Call:

python
Copy
```python
from unittest.mock import patch
import requests

def fetch_data():
    response = requests.get('https://api.example.com/data')
    return response.json()

def test_fetch_data():
    with patch('requests.get') as mock_get:
        mock_get.return_value.json.return_value = {'key': 'value'}
```

```
result = fetch_data()
assert result == {'key': 'value'}
```

In this example, patch() is used to replace the requests.get() method with a mock that returns predefined data. This allows the test to simulate an external API response without actually making a network request.

3. Mocking Database Calls

When testing APIs that interact with a database, you can mock database queries to ensure that tests don't depend on a live database.

Example of Mocking Database Queries with SQLAlchemy:

python

Copy

```
from unittest.mock import patch
from your_app import User

def test_user_query():
    with patch.object(User.query, 'filter_by') as mock_query:
        mock_query.return_value.first.return_value = User(username='mockuser')
        user = User.query.filter_by(username='mockuser').first()
        assert user.username == 'mockuser'
```

This mocks the filter_by() method of SQLAlchemy's query object, so the test doesn't require a real database connection. Instead, it returns a mock user object.

4. Combining Unit Tests, Integration Tests, and Mocking

- **Unit tests** should test individual components (e.g., route handlers, functions).

162

- **Integration tests** should test how components work together, such as interacting with a database or external services.
- **Mocking** external dependencies ensures that integration tests remain fast and do not require actual external systems.

9.4 End-to-End Testing with Postman

End-to-End (E2E) testing is a type of testing that simulates a real-world scenario to ensure that all components of your application work together as expected. Unlike unit tests, which focus on individual components, E2E tests check the functionality of the entire application from the user's perspective. **Postman** is a popular tool for API testing, allowing developers to easily send requests and validate responses.

1. Why Use Postman for End-to-End Testing?

Postman is a powerful tool for manually testing your API and performing automated E2E tests. It provides a user-friendly interface to send requests, validate responses, and organize tests. Here's why Postman is great for E2E testing:

- **Easy to Use**: The intuitive interface makes it simple to send requests to your API and inspect responses.
- **Test Automation**: Postman allows you to write tests using JavaScript, making it easy to automate your API tests and integrate them with continuous integration (CI) pipelines.
- **Environment Variables**: Postman allows you to create environments with variables, making it easier to test the same API with different configurations (e.g., development, staging, production).
- **Collections**: You can organize requests into collections, which can be shared with teams for collaboration.

2. Setting Up Postman for API Testing

You can begin testing your Flask API with Postman by setting up a new request:

- **Step 1: Create a New Request**: Open Postman and create a new request by clicking "New" and then "Request".
- **Step 2: Configure the Request**: Set the HTTP method (GET, POST, PUT, DELETE, etc.) and enter the endpoint URL (e.g., http://localhost:5000/api/resource).
- **Step 3: Add Request Body** (for POST/PUT requests): Under the "Body" tab, you can select the data format (e.g., JSON) and provide the request payload.
- **Step 4: Send the Request**: Click "Send" to send the request to your Flask API.
- **Step 5: Inspect the Response**: Postman will display the response body, headers, and status code.

3. Writing Tests in Postman

Postman allows you to write tests using JavaScript in the "Tests" tab. You can use Postman's built-in assertions (e.g., pm.response.to.have.status(200)) to validate the response.

Example: Testing a GET Request

javascript

Copy

```
// Test that the response status is 200 OK

pm.test("Status is OK", function () {

    pm.response.to.have.status(200);

});
```

164

```
// Test that the response body contains the expected message

pm.test("Message is correct", function () {

    var jsonData = pm.response.json();

    pm.expect(jsonData.message).to.eql("Hello, World!");

});
```

In this example:

- The first test checks that the response status is 200 OK.
- The second test ensures that the response JSON contains the expected message.

4. Automating E2E Tests with Postman Collection Runner

Postman's Collection Runner allows you to run a series of requests and tests automatically. This is useful for running a full suite of E2E tests to validate that your API works as expected.

Steps to Run Tests in Collection Runner:

1. Create a collection in Postman by adding multiple requests.
2. Click the "Runner" button at the top of the screen.
3. Choose the collection and environment.
4. Click "Run" to execute all requests in the collection and view the results.

By running tests in bulk, you can ensure that your entire API is functioning as expected.

9.5 Flask Debugging Tools and Techniques

Debugging is an essential part of developing Flask APIs, allowing you to identify and fix issues before they impact users. Flask provides built-in debugging tools, and there are additional tools and techniques you can use to streamline the debugging process.

1. Flask Debug Mode

Flask has a built-in debug mode that provides detailed error messages and automatically reloads the server when changes are made to the code. You can enable debug mode by setting the FLASK_ENV environment variable to development.

Enable Debug Mode:

bash

Copy

```
export FLASK_ENV=development
```

This will enable Flask's built-in debugger, which provides more detailed error reports when an exception occurs.

2. Flask Debugger

When an error occurs in Flask, the default debugger shows an interactive traceback in the browser, allowing you to inspect variables and step through the code. This can be invaluable when trying to identify the cause of an error.

Example of a Flask Error Page in Debug Mode:

- The debugger provides a stack trace of the error and highlights the exact line where the error occurred.

- It also allows you to inspect local variables, helping you understand the context of the error.

3. Logging in Flask

In addition to the Flask debugger, **logging** is an essential tool for debugging in production. By default, Flask logs error messages to the console, but you can configure Flask to log messages to a file or an external logging service.

Setting Up Logging in Flask:

python

Copy

```python
import logging


app = Flask(__name__)


# Set up logging
logging.basicConfig(level=logging.DEBUG)

app.logger.setLevel(logging.DEBUG)


@app.route('/some_route')

def some_route():

    app.logger.debug("This is a debug message")
```

167

```
app.logger.info("This is an info message")

return "Check your logs!"
```

In this example:

- The logging.basicConfig() method configures the logging settings.
- app.logger.debug() and app.logger.info() log messages at different levels.

4. Debugging External API Requests

When interacting with external APIs, debugging can be more challenging. Use **Flask-Logging** or **requests logging** to capture HTTP request and response data.

Example: Logging HTTP Requests with Requests Library

python

Copy

```
import requests

import logging


logging.basicConfig(level=logging.DEBUG)


response = requests.get('https://api.example.com/data')

logging.debug(f'Response: {response.status_code} - {response.text}')
```

168

This will log the HTTP response status and content, helping you debug external API calls.

9.6 Continuous Integration for Flask Projects

Continuous Integration (CI) is a development practice where code changes are automatically built, tested, and integrated into the project. Setting up CI ensures that your Flask API is consistently tested and deployed with minimal manual intervention, improving code quality and reducing errors.

1. Benefits of Continuous Integration

- **Automated Testing**: Every time you push changes to your repository, automated tests run to ensure that the application is functioning correctly.
- **Faster Development**: CI ensures that bugs are caught early in the development process, which speeds up development and improves quality.
- **Collaborative Development**: With CI, team members can work on different parts of the application simultaneously, knowing that changes will be automatically tested and integrated.

2. Setting Up Continuous Integration for Flask

To set up CI for your Flask project, you can use CI services such as **GitHub Actions**, **Travis CI**, or **CircleCI**. These services integrate with your repository and run tests on each commit or pull request.

Example: Setting Up GitHub Actions for Flask

1. Create a .github/workflows directory in your project.
2. Create a configuration file like python-app.yml for GitHub Actions.

yaml

Copy

```yaml
name: Flask CI

on: [push, pull_request]

jobs:
  test:
    runs-on: ubuntu-latest
    steps:
      - name: Checkout code
        uses: actions/checkout@v2

      - name: Set up Python
        uses: actions/setup-python@v2
        with:
          python-version: '3.8'

      - name: Install dependencies
```

```
run: |

  python -m pip install --upgrade pip

  pip install -r requirements.txt


- name: Run tests

  run: |

    pytest
```

In this example:

- **actions/checkout@v2** checks out the code.
- **actions/setup-python@v2** sets up the Python environment.
- The tests are run using **pytest** to ensure everything works correctly.

3. Automating Deployments

CI can also be configured to automatically deploy your Flask API to a production server once tests pass. This can be done using services like **Heroku**, **AWS**, or **Google Cloud Platform**.

9.7 Summary & What's Next

In this chapter, we covered the essential techniques for testing and debugging Flask APIs:

- **End-to-End Testing with Postman**: We explored how to perform manual and automated E2E tests with Postman to ensure that your API functions correctly.
- **Flask Debugging Tools**: We learned how to enable Flask's debug mode, use logging for troubleshooting, and debug external API requests.
- **Continuous Integration**: We discussed how to set up Continuous Integration for Flask projects to automate testing, improve collaboration, and ensure high code quality.

In the next chapter, we will focus on **API Versioning and Documentation**, covering best practices for versioning your API to maintain compatibility with existing clients and providing clear and comprehensive documentation for developers.

Chapter 10: API Deployment and Best Practices

10.1 Preparing Your Flask API for Production

Before deploying your Flask API to production, it is crucial to ensure that it is optimized for performance, security, and scalability. Proper preparation will help you avoid common issues, such as slow response times, security vulnerabilities, or crashes under high traffic. In this section, we will walk through the essential steps to prepare your Flask API for production.

1. Set Flask to Production Mode

Flask runs in **development mode** by default, which provides helpful error messages and debugging tools. However, this is not suitable for a production environment. In production, Flask should be configured to run in **production mode**, which disables debugging and enhances performance.

To set Flask to production mode:

bash
Copy
```
export FLASK_ENV=production
```

This disables Flask's debug mode and improves the app's performance by not enabling automatic reloading and detailed error pages.

2. Use a Production-Ready Web Server

In development, Flask's built-in web server (flask run) is sufficient, but it is not designed for production use. For production, you should use a robust, scalable web

173

server like **Gunicorn** or **uWSGI**, which can handle multiple requests simultaneously and is optimized for production environments.

Example: Installing Gunicorn

bash
Copy
```
pip install gunicorn
```

Running Flask with Gunicorn:

bash
Copy
```
gunicorn -w 4 myapp:app
```

- -w 4 specifies the number of worker processes to handle requests (4 workers in this case).
- myapp:app refers to your Flask application (app is the Flask instance in myapp.py).

3. Enable Logging

In production, logging is essential for tracking errors and monitoring application performance. You should configure logging to capture detailed information about requests, errors, and system status.

Configuring Logging in Flask:

python
Copy
```
import logging
from logging.handlers import RotatingFileHandler
```

```
app = Flask(__name__)

# Set up a rotating file handler to store logs
handler = RotatingFileHandler('app.log', maxBytes=10000, backupCount=3)
handler.setLevel(logging.INFO)
app.logger.addHandler(handler)

@app.route('/')
def hello_world():
    app.logger.info('Hello world route accessed')
    return "Hello, World!"
```

In this example:

- A **RotatingFileHandler** is used to store logs in a file that rotates after reaching a size limit.
- The log level is set to **INFO**, which captures important messages.

4. Use Environment Variables for Configuration

Sensitive information such as API keys, database credentials, or secret keys should never be hard-coded in your code. Use **environment variables** to store these values securely.

Example: Setting Up Environment Variables

bash

Copy

```
export FLASK_SECRET_KEY='your_secret_key'
export DATABASE_URI='your_database_uri'
```

In your Flask app:

python
Copy
```
import os
app.config['SECRET_KEY'] = os.getenv('FLASK_SECRET_KEY')
app.config['SQLALCHEMY_DATABASE_URI'] = os.getenv('DATABASE_URI')
```

5. Optimize Performance

In production, your API must be optimized to handle high traffic efficiently. Here are some tips for optimizing performance:

- **Caching**: Use **Redis** or **Memcached** to cache responses or database queries, reducing the load on your server and database.
- **Compression**: Enable **GZIP compression** for responses to reduce bandwidth usage and improve load times.
- **Database Optimization**: Use efficient database queries, apply indexes, and limit the amount of data returned by queries to minimize database load.

10.2 Deploying Flask APIs on Popular Platforms (Heroku, AWS, DigitalOcean)

Once your Flask API is production-ready, it's time to deploy it. There are several platforms available for deploying Flask APIs, including **Heroku**, **AWS**, and **DigitalOcean**. In this section, we'll cover how to deploy Flask APIs on each of these popular platforms.

1. Deploying Flask on Heroku

Heroku is a popular Platform-as-a-Service (PaaS) provider that simplifies the deployment process, offering a wide range of tools to deploy and scale applications.

Step 1: Install Heroku CLI First, install the **Heroku CLI** by following the instructions on Heroku's official website.

Step 2: Create a Procfile Heroku requires a Procfile to determine how to run the application. Create a Procfile in the root directory of your project with the following content:

makefile
Copy

```
web: gunicorn myapp:app
```

This tells Heroku to use **Gunicorn** to run the Flask app (myapp:app).

Step 3: Initialize Git Repository If your project is not already in a Git repository, initialize one:

bash
Copy

```
git init
git add .
git commit -m "Initial commit"
```

Step 4: Create a Heroku App and Deploy

bash
Copy

```
heroku create
```

```
git push heroku master
```

This will deploy your Flask API to Heroku.

Step 5: Open the App After the deployment, you can open your app by running:

bash

Copy

```
heroku open
```

2. Deploying Flask on AWS (Amazon Web Services)

AWS offers several ways to deploy a Flask API, including **Elastic Beanstalk** and **EC2** instances.

Step 1: Create an Elastic Beanstalk Environment

- First, install the **AWS CLI** and configure it using your AWS credentials.
- Use the Elastic Beanstalk CLI to deploy your application.

bash

Copy

```
eb init -p python-3.8 my-flask-app
eb create my-flask-app-env
eb open
```

Elastic Beanstalk automatically handles provisioning, load balancing, and scaling.

3. Deploying Flask on DigitalOcean

DigitalOcean provides scalable virtual private servers called **droplets**, which are ideal for deploying Flask applications.

Step 1: Create a Droplet

- Sign in to DigitalOcean and create a droplet using a Linux distribution (e.g., Ubuntu).
- SSH into your droplet using the IP address provided.

Step 2: Set Up the Server Install necessary packages, such as **Python**, **Nginx**, and **Gunicorn**:

bash

Copy

```
sudo apt update
sudo apt install python3-pip python3-dev nginx
pip3 install gunicorn
```

Step 3: Configure Gunicorn and Nginx Create a Gunicorn service file and configure Nginx as a reverse proxy to forward HTTP requests to Gunicorn.

Step 4: Run Your Flask API Start Gunicorn with your Flask app and configure Nginx to serve the API:

bash

Copy

```
gunicorn --workers 4 myapp:app
```

Step 5: Open Your App Once everything is set up, you can access your Flask API via the droplet's public IP address.

179

10.3 Containerizing Flask APIs with Docker

Docker is a platform for developing, shipping, and running applications in containers. Containers are lightweight, portable, and ensure that your application runs consistently across different environments. Containerizing your Flask API makes it easy to deploy, scale, and manage the application.

1. Why Use Docker?

- **Consistency**: Docker ensures that the app runs consistently in any environment (e.g., local development, staging, production).
- **Isolation**: Docker containers provide an isolated environment for your application, reducing conflicts between dependencies and other applications.
- **Portability**: Docker containers can run on any machine that has Docker installed, making deployment across platforms easy.

2. Creating a Dockerfile for Flask

A Dockerfile is a text document that contains instructions to build a Docker image for your application. Here's how to create a Dockerfile for your Flask API:

Step 1: Create a Dockerfile

dockerfile

Copy

```
# Use the official Python image as a base
FROM python:3.8-slim

# Set the working directory inside the container
WORKDIR /app

# Copy the application files to the container
```

```
COPY . /app

# Install the dependencies
RUN pip install -r requirements.txt

# Expose the application port
EXPOSE 5000

# Run the Flask app using Gunicorn
CMD ["gunicorn", "-b", "0.0.0.0:5000", "myapp:app"]
```

Step 2: Build the Docker Image

bash

Copy

```
docker build -t flask-api .
```

Step 3: Run the Docker Container

bash

Copy

```
docker run -p 5000:5000 flask-api
```

This will start the Flask app inside a container and make it accessible on port 5000.

3. Deploying Docker Containers to Cloud Providers

Once your Flask app is containerized, you can deploy it to cloud providers like **AWS ECS**, **Google Kubernetes Engine (GKE)**, or **DigitalOcean Kubernetes**. These platforms support containerized applications and make it easy to scale your Flask API.

181

10.4 Continuous Deployment with GitLab CI/CD

Continuous Deployment (CD) is the practice of automatically deploying code to production after passing tests. With **GitLab CI/CD**, you can automate your deployment pipeline and ensure that your Flask API is deployed quickly, reliably, and consistently. GitLab CI/CD allows you to set up automated testing, building, and deployment processes directly from your GitLab repository.

1. Why Use Continuous Deployment?

- **Faster Deployment**: CD allows you to push new features, fixes, and improvements to production quickly without manual intervention.
- **Reliability**: By automating the deployment process, CD ensures that your application is deployed the same way every time, reducing the risk of human error.
- **Consistency**: CD ensures that your development, staging, and production environments are kept in sync, as the same process is used for deployment across all environments.

2. Setting Up GitLab CI/CD for Flask

To set up GitLab CI/CD for your Flask application, follow these steps:

Step 1: Create a .gitlab-ci.yml **File** GitLab CI/CD uses a .gitlab-ci.yml file, which defines the build, test, and deploy pipelines. Here's an example configuration for deploying a Flask API:

```yaml
Copy
stages:
  - build
```

```yaml
  - test
  - deploy

# Build stage: Install dependencies
build:
  stage: build
  image: python:3.8
  script:
    - pip install -r requirements.txt

# Test stage: Run tests using pytest
test:
  stage: test
  image: python:3.8
  script:
    - pip install -r requirements.txt
    - pytest

# Deploy stage: Deploy to the production server
deploy:
  stage: deploy
  script:
    - ssh user@yourserver.com 'cd /path/to/your/app && git pull && systemctl restart flask-app'
  only:
    - master
```

Explanation:

- **Build**: Installs the required dependencies using pip.

183

- **Test**: Runs unit tests using pytest to ensure that the API functions as expected.
- **Deploy**: Deploys the latest changes to the production server by pulling the latest code and restarting the app using systemctl.

Step 2: Configure SSH Access For deployment to a remote server, you'll need SSH access. Ensure that your GitLab CI/CD pipeline has SSH keys set up so that it can securely connect to your production server.

Step 3: Trigger the Pipeline Once your .gitlab-ci.yml file is in place, GitLab CI/CD will automatically run the pipeline every time changes are pushed to the repository. The pipeline will run tests, build the application, and deploy it if everything passes.

3. Benefits of GitLab CI/CD

- **Automated Deployment**: Automates the entire deployment pipeline, from testing to production deployment.
- **Faster Feedback**: Get immediate feedback on code quality and functionality through automated testing.
- **Consistency Across Environments**: Ensure that your deployment process is the same for all environments (development, staging, production).

10.5 Using Nginx and Gunicorn for High-Performance Flask APIs

For high-performance Flask API deployments, using a combination of **Nginx** and **Gunicorn** is a best practice. **Gunicorn** is a lightweight WSGI server for Python web applications, and **Nginx** is a powerful reverse proxy and load balancer that helps serve static files and distribute traffic efficiently across Gunicorn workers.

1. Why Use Nginx and Gunicorn?

- **Gunicorn** is designed to handle Python applications efficiently. It can manage multiple requests in parallel, making it suitable for production environments.
- **Nginx** serves as a reverse proxy server that handles client requests and forwards them to Gunicorn. It also handles static files, improving performance by offloading this work from Gunicorn.

2. Setting Up Gunicorn

Gunicorn is easy to set up. First, install it in your Flask project:

bash
Copy
```
pip install gunicorn
```

Then, run your Flask app with Gunicorn:

bash
Copy
```
gunicorn -w 4 myapp:app
```

Here, -w 4 specifies that Gunicorn should use 4 worker processes to handle requests, which allows it to serve multiple requests simultaneously.

3. Configuring Nginx as a Reverse Proxy

Next, set up **Nginx** as a reverse proxy for your Flask API. Nginx will handle incoming HTTP requests and forward them to Gunicorn, which will process them.

Step 1: Install Nginx

bash

Copy

```bash
sudo apt-get install nginx
```

Step 2: Configure Nginx Create a new Nginx configuration file for your Flask app. This file should define how Nginx should route traffic to your Gunicorn server.

Example Nginx Configuration:

nginx

Copy

```nginx
server {
    listen 80;
    server_name myflaskapp.com;

    location / {
        proxy_pass http://127.0.0.1:8000;  # Forward requests to Gunicorn
        proxy_set_header Host $host;
        proxy_set_header X-Real-IP $remote_addr;
        proxy_set_header X-Forwarded-For $proxy_add_x_forwarded_for;
    }

    location /static {
        alias /path/to/your/app/static;
    }
}
```

This configuration ensures that Nginx forwards incoming requests to Gunicorn running on localhost:8000. It also serves static files directly, which is more efficient than having Gunicorn handle static content.

Step 3: Restart Nginx After configuring Nginx, restart it to apply the changes:

bash

Copy

sudo systemctl restart nginx

4. Benefits of Nginx and Gunicorn

- **Load Balancing**: Nginx can distribute traffic across multiple Gunicorn workers or even multiple instances of your Flask app, improving scalability and availability.
- **Performance**: Nginx efficiently serves static files and handles HTTP requests, leaving Gunicorn to focus on running the Flask application.
- **Security**: Nginx can act as a barrier between the outside world and your application, helping protect your Flask API from direct exposure to the internet.

10.6 Monitoring and Logging in Production Environments

Monitoring and logging are critical for maintaining the health of your Flask API in production. Proper monitoring allows you to detect issues early, track the performance of your API, and troubleshoot problems efficiently. Logging helps capture detailed information about your app's behavior, making it easier to diagnose issues.

1. Setting Up Monitoring

Monitoring ensures that your Flask API is running smoothly in production. Common monitoring tools include **Prometheus**, **Grafana**, and **New Relic**.

- **Prometheus**: Collects metrics from your Flask application, such as request times, error rates, and resource usage.
- **Grafana**: Visualizes the data collected by Prometheus, providing insightful dashboards for tracking the performance of your application.
- **New Relic**: Provides real-time performance monitoring, tracking everything from application performance to user interactions.

2. Logging in Production

In production, you should configure your Flask application to log important events, errors, and performance metrics. Use **Flask's built-in logging** or an external service like **Loggly**, **Sentry**, or **Datadog** for more advanced logging.

Example: Logging Errors in Flask

python
Copy

```
import logging
from logging.handlers import RotatingFileHandler

app = Flask(__name__)

# Set up a rotating file handler to store logs
handler = RotatingFileHandler('app.log', maxBytes=10000, backupCount=3)
handler.setLevel(logging.INFO)
app.logger.addHandler(handler)
```

188

```
@app.route('/')
def hello_world():
    app.logger.info('Hello world route accessed')
    return "Hello, World!"
```

In this example, logs are stored in a file and rotated after reaching a certain size. You can log different levels of events (e.g., **INFO**, **WARNING**, **ERROR**) based on their importance.

3. Using Distributed Logging Systems

For larger applications, you might need to aggregate logs from multiple instances. Use **centralized logging systems** like **ELK Stack** (Elasticsearch, Logstash, Kibana) or **Fluentd** to collect and analyze logs across all your API instances.

Example with Fluentd:

- **Fluentd** collects logs from your Flask app and sends them to an external service (e.g., Elasticsearch or Loggly).
- **Kibana** visualizes the logs and provides powerful search capabilities.

4. Setting Up Alerts

In addition to monitoring, set up **alerting** to notify you when something goes wrong. Common alerting systems include:

- **PagerDuty**
- **Slack**
- **Email Notifications**

For example, you can configure New Relic or Prometheus to send alerts if your API response time exceeds a certain threshold or if the error rate spikes.

10.7 Summary & What's Next

In this chapter, we discussed several critical aspects of deploying Flask APIs:

- **Continuous Deployment with GitLab CI/CD**: We covered how to automate your deployment process using GitLab CI/CD pipelines, ensuring faster and more reliable deployments.
- **Nginx and Gunicorn for High-Performance APIs**: We learned how to set up Nginx as a reverse proxy to serve your Flask app via Gunicorn, ensuring high performance and scalability.
- **Monitoring and Logging in Production**: We explored the importance of monitoring and logging for maintaining the health of your Flask API in production and using tools like Prometheus, Grafana, and centralized logging systems.

Next, we will focus on **API Versioning and Documentation**, where we will discuss how to manage API versions effectively and provide detailed, clear documentation for developers and users.

Chapter 11: Flask in the Real World

11.1 Real-World API Case Study: Building an E-Commerce API

Building an API for an e-commerce platform requires handling various functionalities, including user authentication, managing products, processing orders, and integrating payment systems. In this section, we will go through a case study of building an e-commerce API with Flask, covering key components such as product management, user authentication, and order processing.

1. Features of an E-Commerce API

An e-commerce API should support the following key features:

- **User Authentication and Authorization**: Users should be able to register, log in, and authenticate to perform actions like placing orders.
- **Product Management**: Products should be able to be created, updated, deleted, and viewed.
- **Cart and Order Management**: Users should be able to add items to their cart, modify quantities, and place orders.
- **Payment Integration**: Integration with a payment gateway (e.g., Stripe, PayPal) to handle transactions securely.

2. Setting Up Flask for E-Commerce

Let's start by setting up a simple structure for the e-commerce API using **Flask**, **SQLAlchemy**, and **Flask-JWT-Extended** for JWT-based authentication.

Step 1: Install Required Packages

bash

Copy

```bash
pip install Flask Flask-SQLAlchemy Flask-JWT-Extended
```

Step 2: Define Models for Users, Products, and Orders

python

Copy

```python
from flask import Flask, request, jsonify
from flask_sqlalchemy import SQLAlchemy
from flask_jwt_extended import JWTManager, create_access_token, jwt_required

app = Flask(__name__)
app.config['SQLALCHEMY_DATABASE_URI'] = 'sqlite:///ecommerce.db'
app.config['SECRET_KEY'] = 'your_secret_key'
db = SQLAlchemy(app)
jwt = JWTManager(app)

# User model
class User(db.Model):
    id = db.Column(db.Integer, primary_key=True)
    username = db.Column(db.String(80), unique=True, nullable=False)
    password = db.Column(db.String(120), nullable=False)

# Product model
class Product(db.Model):
    id = db.Column(db.Integer, primary_key=True)
    name = db.Column(db.String(80), nullable=False)
```

```python
    price = db.Column(db.Float, nullable=False)

# Order model
class Order(db.Model):
    id = db.Column(db.Integer, primary_key=True)
    user_id = db.Column(db.Integer, db.ForeignKey('user.id'), nullable=False)
    total_amount = db.Column(db.Float, nullable=False)
    user = db.relationship('User', backref='orders', lazy=True)

# Initialize the database
with app.app_context():
    db.create_all()
```

In this example:

- The **User** model stores user information (e.g., username, password).
- The **Product** model stores product information (e.g., name, price).
- The **Order** model links a user to their orders, with a reference to the total amount.

Step 3: User Authentication We'll create a route for user registration and login, using **JWT** for authentication.

python

Copy

```python
@app.route('/register', methods=['POST'])
def register():
    data = request.get_json()
    new_user = User(username=data['username'], password=data['password'])
    db.session.add(new_user)
    db.session.commit()
```

```python
    return jsonify({'message': 'User registered successfully'}), 201

@app.route('/login', methods=['POST'])
def login():
    data = request.get_json()
    user = User.query.filter_by(username=data['username']).first()
    if user and user.password == data['password']:
        access_token = create_access_token(identity=user.id)
        return jsonify({'access_token': access_token}), 200
    return jsonify({'message': 'Invalid credentials'}), 401
```

In this code:

- /register allows new users to sign up.
- /login authenticates the user and returns a JWT access token.

Step 4: Product Management Now, let's add product management functionality, including adding, viewing, and deleting products.

python
Copy

```python
@app.route('/products', methods=['GET'])
def get_products():
    products = Product.query.all()
    return jsonify([{'id': p.id, 'name': p.name, 'price': p.price} for p in products])

@app.route('/products', methods=['POST'])
@jwt_required()
def add_product():
    data = request.get_json()
    new_product = Product(name=data['name'], price=data['price'])
```

194

```python
    db.session.add(new_product)
    db.session.commit()
    return jsonify({'message': 'Product added successfully'}), 201

@app.route('/products/<int:id>', methods=['DELETE'])
@jwt_required()
def delete_product(id):
    product = Product.query.get(id)
    if product:
        db.session.delete(product)
        db.session.commit()
        return jsonify({'message': 'Product deleted successfully'}), 200
    return jsonify({'message': 'Product not found'}), 404
```

This code allows authenticated users to add and delete products, as well as view all available products.

Step 5: Order Management Now, let's add the functionality to create and manage orders.

python
Copy

```python
@app.route('/order', methods=['POST'])
@jwt_required()
def create_order():
    data = request.get_json()
    user_id = get_jwt_identity()
    products = data['products']

    # Calculate total amount (assuming we have a product ID list)
```

```
total_amount = sum([Product.query.get(pid).price for pid in products])

new_order = Order(user_id=user_id, total_amount=total_amount)
db.session.add(new_order)
db.session.commit()

return jsonify({'message': 'Order placed successfully', 'order_id': new_order.id}), 201
```

In this example:

- The **create_order** route allows authenticated users to place an order by specifying a list of product IDs.

2. Best Practices for Building E-Commerce APIs

- **Authentication**: Always secure sensitive endpoints with authentication (JWT or OAuth).
- **Error Handling**: Properly handle errors and return meaningful error messages.
- **Payment Integration**: Integrate with payment gateways like Stripe or PayPal to process payments securely.
- **Security**: Use HTTPS to encrypt data and protect user information.
- **Scalability**: Use caching (e.g., Redis) and consider deploying your app with load balancing to handle high traffic.

11.2 Building a Social Media API with Flask

Social media platforms typically involve user profiles, posts, comments, and likes, along with authentication and authorization. In this section, we will build a basic social media API that allows users to post messages, view profiles, and follow each other.

1. Features of a Social Media API

- **User Authentication**: Users should be able to register, log in, and authenticate to post messages and follow others.
- **Profile Management**: Users should have profiles that include basic information.
- **Posts**: Users should be able to post messages and view posts from others.
- **Following and Followers**: Users can follow and be followed by other users.

2. Setting Up the Social Media API

Let's create a simple Flask app with user authentication, post management, and follow functionality.

Step 1: Define Models for Users, Posts, and Followers

python

Copy

```python
class User(db.Model):
    id = db.Column(db.Integer, primary_key=True)
    username = db.Column(db.String(80), unique=True, nullable=False)
    password = db.Column(db.String(120), nullable=False)
    posts = db.relationship('Post', backref='author', lazy=True)
    followers = db.relationship('Follower', backref='followed', lazy=True)


class Post(db.Model):
    id = db.Column(db.Integer, primary_key=True)
    content = db.Column(db.String(500), nullable=False)
    user_id = db.Column(db.Integer, db.ForeignKey('user.id'), nullable=False)


class Follower(db.Model):
    id = db.Column(db.Integer, primary_key=True)
    follower_id = db.Column(db.Integer, db.ForeignKey('user.id'), nullable=False)
```

197

```python
followed_id = db.Column(db.Integer, db.ForeignKey('user.id'), nullable=False)
```

Step 2: Implement Routes for User Registration, Login, Posting, and Following

python

Copy

```python
@app.route('/register', methods=['POST'])
def register():
    data = request.get_json()
    new_user = User(username=data['username'], password=data['password'])
    db.session.add(new_user)
    db.session.commit()
    return jsonify({'message': 'User registered successfully'}), 201


@app.route('/post', methods=['POST'])
@jwt_required()
def create_post():
    data = request.get_json()
    user_id = get_jwt_identity()
    new_post = Post(content=data['content'], user_id=user_id)
    db.session.add(new_post)
    db.session.commit()
    return jsonify({'message': 'Post created successfully'}), 201


@app.route('/follow/<int:followed_id>', methods=['POST'])
@jwt_required()
def follow_user(followed_id):
    user_id = get_jwt_identity()
    if user_id != followed_id:
        new_follow = Follower(follower_id=user_id, followed_id=followed_id)
```

```
db.session.add(new_follow)
db.session.commit()
return jsonify({'message': f'Now following user {followed_id}'}), 200
return jsonify({'message': 'You cannot follow yourself'}), 400
```

This basic example allows users to register, post content, and follow other users. You can expand it further to include likes, comments, and user profiles.

11.3 IoT APIs with Flask: Connecting Devices to the Web

The Internet of Things (IoT) involves connecting devices to the internet to collect and share data. Flask is well-suited for building APIs that interact with IoT devices, enabling communication between sensors, actuators, and web-based applications.

1. Features of an IoT API

- **Device Registration**: Devices should be able to register with the API.
- **Data Collection**: Devices should send data (e.g., sensor readings) to the API.
- **Real-time Communication**: The API should support real-time data processing, such as sending alerts based on sensor readings.
- **Control Devices**: The API should allow users to control or configure devices remotely.

2. Setting Up the IoT API

Let's create an API to handle IoT devices, including registration, data submission, and real-time communication.

Step 1: Define Models for Devices and Data

python

Copy

```python
class Device(db.Model):
    id = db.Column(db.Integer, primary_key=True)
    name = db.Column(db.String(80), nullable=False)
    data = db.relationship('DeviceData', backref='device', lazy=True)


class DeviceData(db.Model):
    id = db.Column(db.Integer, primary_key=True)
    value = db.Column(db.Float, nullable=False)
    timestamp = db.Column(db.DateTime, default=datetime.utcnow)
    device_id = db.Column(db.Integer, db.ForeignKey('device.id'), nullable=False)
```

Step 2: Implement Routes for Device Registration and Data Collection

python

Copy

```python
@app.route('/register_device', methods=['POST'])
def register_device():
    data = request.get_json()
    new_device = Device(name=data['name'])
    db.session.add(new_device)
    db.session.commit()
    return jsonify({'message': 'Device registered successfully'}), 201


@app.route('/device_data', methods=['POST'])
def submit_device_data():
    data = request.get_json()
```

```
device = Device.query.get(data['device_id'])
if device:
    new_data = DeviceData(value=data['value'], device_id=device.id)
    db.session.add(new_data)
    db.session.commit()
    return jsonify({'message': 'Data submitted successfully'}), 201
return jsonify({'message': 'Device not found'}), 404
```

In this example:

- The **Device** model stores information about each IoT device.
- The **DeviceData** model stores the sensor readings submitted by the device.

3. Real-Time Communication for IoT

To handle real-time data streaming from IoT devices, you can integrate **WebSockets** using **Flask-SocketIO**. This allows the server to push data updates to clients as soon as new data is received from the devices.

11.4 Flask for Microservices: Breaking Down Complex Systems

Microservices is an architectural style that decomposes a large, monolithic application into smaller, independent services that communicate over a network. Flask is an excellent choice for building microservices due to its lightweight nature, simplicity, and flexibility. In this section, we'll explore how to break down a complex system into microservices using Flask.

1. Why Use Flask for Microservices?

Flask is well-suited for microservices because:

- **Lightweight**: Flask is minimalistic and allows you to build small, self-contained services with minimal overhead.
- **Flexibility**: Flask doesn't enforce any specific architecture or components, so you can customize your microservices as needed.
- **Scalability**: Since microservices are small, independent components, they can be scaled horizontally to handle increased traffic by adding more instances of each service.

2. Breaking Down a Monolithic Application into Microservices

Let's say you have an e-commerce application with a monolithic architecture, and you want to split it into microservices. You could break the system into the following services:

- **User Service**: Manages user accounts, authentication, and authorization.
- **Product Service**: Handles the catalog of products, including product details, pricing, and inventory.
- **Order Service**: Manages user orders, including placing orders, updating order statuses, and calculating totals.
- **Payment Service**: Handles payment processing and interactions with external payment gateways.

Each of these services can be implemented as separate Flask applications with their own APIs.

3. Example: Setting Up a User Service with Flask

Here's how you might set up the **User Service** using Flask:

Step 1: Define the User Model

python

Copy

```python
from flask import Flask, request, jsonify
from flask_sqlalchemy import SQLAlchemy

app = Flask(__name__)
app.config['SQLALCHEMY_DATABASE_URI'] = 'sqlite:///users.db'
db = SQLAlchemy(app)

class User(db.Model):
    id = db.Column(db.Integer, primary_key=True)
    username = db.Column(db.String(80), unique=True, nullable=False)
    password = db.Column(db.String(120), nullable=False)

db.create_all()
```

Step 2: Implement Routes for Registration and Login

python

Copy

```python
@app.route('/register', methods=['POST'])
def register():
    data = request.get_json()
    new_user = User(username=data['username'], password=data['password'])
    db.session.add(new_user)
    db.session.commit()
    return jsonify({'message': 'User registered successfully'}), 201


@app.route('/login', methods=['POST'])
def login():
    data = request.get_json()
    user = User.query.filter_by(username=data['username']).first()
    if user and user.password == data['password']:
        return jsonify({'message': 'Login successful'}), 200
    return jsonify({'message': 'Invalid credentials'}), 401
```

Step 3: Run the User Service

bash

Copy

```
flask run
```

This service will handle user registration and login. You can replicate this for the other services in the system.

4. Service Communication

Microservices typically communicate over HTTP, using RESTful APIs, or asynchronously through message brokers like **RabbitMQ** or **Kafka**. When the **Order Service** needs to access user data, it can call the **User Service** via an HTTP request.

Example: Communicating Between Services (Order Service calling User Service)

python

Copy

```
import requests


@app.route('/order', methods=['POST'])

def create_order():

    user_id = request.json['user_id']

    # Get user details from User Service
```

```
user_response = requests.get(f'http://user-service:5000/user/{user_id}')

if user_response.status_code == 200:

    # Process order...

    return jsonify({'message': 'Order created successfully'}), 201

return jsonify({'message': 'User not found'}), 404
```

In this example, the **Order Service** sends a GET request to the **User Service** to retrieve user details before processing an order.

5. Managing Microservices with Docker

Microservices are often containerized to ensure consistency across different environments. **Docker** makes it easy to package each Flask service into a container, ensuring that each service has the necessary dependencies and runs consistently.

Example: Dockerizing the User Service

1. Create a Dockerfile in the User Service directory:

dockerfile

Copy

```
FROM python:3.8-slim


WORKDIR /app

COPY . /app
```

RUN pip install -r requirements.txt

EXPOSE 5000

CMD ["flask", "run", "--host", "0.0.0.0"]

2. Build and run the Docker container:

bash

Copy

```
docker build -t user-service .

docker run -p 5000:5000 user-service
```

You can replicate this process for other services in your system.

6. Benefits of Using Flask for Microservices

- **Modularity**: Each service is self-contained and can be developed, tested, and deployed independently.
- **Scalability**: Microservices allow each component to be scaled independently, ensuring that resources are allocated efficiently.
- **Resilience**: If one service fails, it doesn't necessarily affect the rest of the system, improving overall reliability.

207

11.5 Best Practices from Real-World Flask Applications

Building real-world Flask applications requires more than just creating endpoints. It involves following best practices that ensure the application is maintainable, scalable, and secure. In this section, we will discuss some key best practices for Flask development.

1. Structure Your Application Properly

Flask is flexible, but that flexibility can lead to messy applications if the project structure is not well planned. Follow a clear structure to keep your code organized and maintainable.

Recommended Flask Project Structure:

bash

Copy

```
/myapp
    /app
        __init__.py
        /models
        /routes
        /templates
        /static
    /config.py
```

/run.py

/requirements.txt

- **models**: Store your data models.
- **routes**: Organize API endpoints.
- **templates**: Store HTML files (if needed).
- **static**: Store static files (CSS, JavaScript).

2. Use Blueprints for Modularization

Flask **Blueprints** allow you to organize your application into smaller, reusable components. For example, you could create a blueprint for the **user authentication** system and another for the **product management** system.

Example:

python

Copy

```python
from flask import Blueprint


auth_bp = Blueprint('auth', __name__)


@auth_bp.route('/login', methods=['POST'])

def login():

    return 'Login Page'
```

In your main application, register the blueprint:

python

Copy

```python
from flask import Flask
from .auth import auth_bp


app = Flask(__name__)
app.register_blueprint(auth_bp, url_prefix='/auth')
```

3. Error Handling

Proper error handling is critical for providing clear feedback to clients. Use **Flask's error handling** system to manage different types of errors (e.g., 404, 500) and return meaningful messages.

python

Copy

```python
@app.errorhandler(404)
def not_found(error):
    return jsonify({'message': 'Resource not found'}), 404
```

4. Secure Your Flask API

Security should be a top priority when developing Flask APIs:

- **Use HTTPS**: Ensure all communication between clients and servers is encrypted.
- **JWT for Authentication**: Use **JWT** for token-based authentication, ensuring secure user sessions.
- **Rate Limiting**: Use Flask extensions like **Flask-Limiter** to limit the number of requests to prevent abuse.

5. Testing and Documentation

- **Unit Testing**: Write tests for all endpoints using **Pytest** or **unittest** to ensure everything functions as expected.
- **API Documentation**: Use tools like **Swagger** or **Flask-RESTPlus** to generate API documentation automatically.

6. Optimize Performance

- **Caching**: Use **Redis** or **Memcached** to cache frequently accessed data and reduce the load on your database.
- **Asynchronous Tasks**: Use **Celery** for handling long-running tasks like email sending or background processing, preventing the API from blocking.

11.6 Summary & What's Next

In this chapter, we explored several real-world applications of Flask:

- **Flask for Microservices**: We learned how to use Flask to break down a monolithic application into smaller, independent services, improving scalability and resilience.

211

- **Best Practices**: We covered key best practices for developing maintainable, scalable, and secure Flask applications, including proper project structure, modularization with blueprints, error handling, and security practices.

In the next chapter, we will focus on **API Versioning and Documentation**, where we will explore how to manage versions of your API and provide comprehensive, user-friendly documentation to help developers interact with your API effectively.

Chapter 12: Advanced Topics in Flask API Development

12.1 Building a GraphQL API with Flask

GraphQL is a query language for APIs and a runtime for executing those queries by using a type system you define for your data. Unlike REST, where each endpoint corresponds to a fixed resource, GraphQL gives clients the ability to request exactly the data they need, which can help reduce over-fetching and under-fetching of data.

1. Why Choose GraphQL?

- **Flexible Queries**: Clients can request exactly what they need, including nested data, without having to make multiple requests to different endpoints.
- **Strong Typing**: GraphQL schemas define the structure of the API, which ensures consistency and predictability in responses.
- **Single Endpoint**: Instead of having many endpoints, GraphQL typically uses a single endpoint to handle various types of requests, reducing the need for multiple routes.

2. Setting Up GraphQL with Flask

To build a GraphQL API with Flask, you'll need the **Graphene** library, which provides integration between Flask and GraphQL.

Step 1: Install Required Packages

bash

Copy

```
pip install Flask graphene graphene-sqlalchemy
```

Step 2: Define Your GraphQL Schema Let's create a basic GraphQL API that allows querying users from a database. For this, you'll define a User model and create a GraphQL query type.

Example Flask Application with GraphQL:

python
Copy
```python
from flask import Flask
from flask_graphql import GraphQLView
from graphene import ObjectType, String, Schema
from graphene_sqlalchemy import SQLAlchemyObjectType,
SQLAlchemyConnectionField
from flask_sqlalchemy import SQLAlchemy

app = Flask(__name__)
app.config['SQLALCHEMY_DATABASE_URI'] = 'sqlite:///mydb.db'
db = SQLAlchemy(app)

# Define the User model
class User(db.Model):
    id = db.Column(db.Integer, primary_key=True)
    name = db.Column(db.String(50))

# Define a GraphQL ObjectType for the User model
class UserType(SQLAlchemyObjectType):
    class Meta:
        model = User
```

```python
# Define the Query class
class Query(ObjectType):
    users = SQLAlchemyConnectionField(UserType.connection)

# Create the schema
schema = Schema(query=Query)

# Add the GraphQL view to Flask
app.add_url_rule('/graphql', view_func=GraphQLView.as_view('graphql',
schema=schema, graphiql=True))

# Run the Flask app
if __name__ == '__main__':
    app.run(debug=True)
```

Explanation:

- **User Model**: Defines a simple SQLAlchemy User model with a name attribute.
- **UserType**: A GraphQL object that maps the User model to GraphQL fields.
- **Query Class**: Defines a GraphQL query for fetching users, which uses SQLAlchemyConnectionField to enable pagination.
- **GraphQLView**: The /graphql endpoint allows users to interact with the GraphQL API using the built-in GraphiQL interface.

Step 3: Querying the API With this setup, you can now query the API using GraphQL queries like:

graphql

Copy

```
{
  users {
```

```
    edges {
      node {
        id
        name
      }
    }
  }
}
```

This query will return a list of users with their id and name.

3. Advantages of GraphQL

- **Efficient Data Fetching**: Clients can request only the data they need, reducing the amount of data transferred over the network.
- **Better Developer Experience**: The strong type system and introspection in GraphQL make it easier to understand and interact with APIs.
- **Flexibility**: GraphQL supports complex queries and allows for easy updates to the schema.

12.2 Using Flask with Kubernetes for Scalability

Kubernetes is an open-source platform for automating deployment, scaling, and operations of containerized applications. It is especially useful for microservices and cloud-native applications where you need to manage and scale multiple services efficiently. In this section, we'll discuss how to deploy Flask APIs on Kubernetes for scalability and high availability.

1. Why Use Kubernetes?

- **Scalability**: Kubernetes makes it easy to scale your Flask API horizontally by adding more instances (pods) to handle increased traffic.
- **High Availability**: Kubernetes ensures that your application is always running, and it automatically restarts failed containers.
- **Load Balancing**: Kubernetes includes built-in load balancing to distribute traffic evenly across all available instances of your Flask app.

2. Dockerizing Your Flask Application

Before deploying your Flask API to Kubernetes, you need to containerize it using **Docker**.

Step 1: Create a Dockerfile for Your Flask App Here's a simple Dockerfile to containerize your Flask application:

dockerfile

Copy

```
FROM python:3.8-slim

WORKDIR /app
COPY . /app

RUN pip install -r requirements.txt

EXPOSE 5000

CMD ["flask", "run", "--host", "0.0.0.0"]
```

Step 2: Build the Docker Image

bash

Copy

```
docker build -t flask-api .
```

Step 3: Run the Docker Container

bash

Copy

```
docker run -p 5000:5000 flask-api
```

At this point, you have a containerized version of your Flask application running locally.

3. Deploying to Kubernetes

Once your Flask API is containerized, you can deploy it to a Kubernetes cluster.

Step 1: Create a Kubernetes Deployment A Kubernetes **Deployment** manages the deployment of your containerized Flask application. It ensures that the desired number of pods are running.

Create a file named flask-api-deployment.yaml with the following content:

yaml

Copy

```
apiVersion: apps/v1
kind: Deployment
metadata:
  name: flask-api
spec:
  replicas: 3
  selector:
```

```
    matchLabels:
      app: flask-api
  template:
    metadata:
      labels:
        app: flask-api
    spec:
      containers:
        - name: flask-api
          image: flask-api:latest
          ports:
            - containerPort: 5000
```

Step 2: Create a Kubernetes Service A **Service** in Kubernetes is used to expose your Flask API to external traffic.

Create a file named flask-api-service.yaml with the following content:

yaml
Copy

```
apiVersion: v1
kind: Service
metadata:
  name: flask-api
spec:
  selector:
    app: flask-api
  ports:
    - protocol: TCP
      port: 80
```

```
    targetPort: 5000
  type: LoadBalancer
```

Step 3: Apply the Deployment and Service Run the following commands to deploy the Flask API and expose it:

bash

Copy

```
kubectl apply -f flask-api-deployment.yaml
kubectl apply -f flask-api-service.yaml
```

Step 4: Access the Flask API Kubernetes will expose your Flask API on a public IP address if you use the LoadBalancer type for the service. You can get the external IP using:

bash

Copy

```
kubectl get services
```

Kubernetes will automatically handle load balancing, scaling, and ensuring high availability for your Flask application.

4. Benefits of Kubernetes for Flask APIs

- **Automatic Scaling**: Kubernetes can automatically scale your Flask application up or down based on traffic.
- **Self-Healing**: Kubernetes automatically restarts containers that fail, ensuring that your application is always available.
- **Efficient Resource Management**: Kubernetes allows you to efficiently manage resources across multiple containers and services, optimizing performance.

12.3 Flask and Serverless Architectures

A **serverless architecture** allows you to run applications without managing the underlying infrastructure. **AWS Lambda** and **Google Cloud Functions** are popular serverless platforms that can run Flask APIs. Serverless computing abstracts away the management of servers and scaling, allowing you to focus on writing code.

1. Why Use Serverless with Flask?

- **No Infrastructure Management**: You don't need to worry about managing servers or scaling.
- **Cost-Effective**: You only pay for the resources you use, which can be more cost-effective than running a dedicated server or virtual machine.
- **Automatic Scaling**: Serverless platforms automatically scale your application based on incoming traffic.

2. Setting Up Flask with AWS Lambda

To use Flask in a serverless environment, you need to adapt it to run on AWS Lambda. This can be done using the **Zappa** or **AWS Serverless Application Model (SAM)** for Flask.

Step 1: Install Zappa Zappa is a Python package that makes it easy to deploy Flask applications to AWS Lambda.

bash

Copy

```
pip install zappa
```

Step 2: Initialize Zappa Run the following command to configure Zappa with your Flask application:

bash

Copy

```
zappa init
```

Zappa will create a zappa_settings.json configuration file.

Step 3: Deploy Your Flask App to AWS Lambda Once you've configured Zappa, deploy your Flask app to AWS Lambda:

bash

Copy

```
zappa deploy production
```

Zappa will automatically package your Flask app, create the necessary AWS Lambda function, and deploy it.

Step 4: Access Your Serverless Flask API Zappa will provide a URL for your Flask API, which you can use to access it over the internet.

3. Benefits of Serverless Architectures for Flask

- **Scalability**: Serverless platforms automatically handle scaling based on incoming requests.
- **No Server Management**: You don't need to manage servers, load balancing, or infrastructure.
- **Cost-Efficiency**: You only pay for the exact amount of computing time your Flask application uses.

12.4 Machine Learning and Flask: Integrating ML Models into APIs

Flask can be an excellent tool for integrating machine learning models into APIs, allowing you to expose the capabilities of your trained models via HTTP requests. This can be useful for building AI-powered services that can be accessed by clients or other systems. In this section, we will explore how to use Flask to serve machine learning models and create an API endpoint for making predictions.

1. Why Use Flask for Machine Learning APIs?

- **Simplicity**: Flask is minimal and easy to set up, making it an ideal choice for quickly creating APIs that expose machine learning models.
- **Flexibility**: Flask allows you to use any machine learning library, whether it's **scikit-learn**, **TensorFlow**, **PyTorch**, or any other model-building framework.
- **Scalability**: Flask can easily be containerized and deployed in scalable environments, such as Kubernetes or cloud platforms.

2. Setting Up Flask to Serve a Machine Learning Model

We'll walk through how to build a Flask API that uses a pre-trained **scikit-learn** model to make predictions.

Step 1: Install Required Libraries

bash

Copy

```
pip install Flask scikit-learn
```

Step 2: Train and Save a Model First, we need to train and save a machine learning model using **scikit-learn**. For simplicity, let's assume we are using a classification model trained on the **Iris dataset**.

python

Copy

```python
import joblib

from sklearn.datasets import load_iris

from sklearn.model_selection import train_test_split

from sklearn.ensemble import RandomForestClassifier


# Load and split the dataset

iris = load_iris()

X_train, X_test, y_train, y_test = train_test_split(iris.data, iris.target, test_size=0.2)


# Train a model

model = RandomForestClassifier()

model.fit(X_train, y_train)


# Save the model

joblib.dump(model, 'iris_model.pkl')
```

224

This code trains a **RandomForestClassifier** on the Iris dataset and saves the trained model to a file (iris_model.pkl).

Step 3: Create the Flask API Now, we'll create a Flask API that loads the saved model and uses it to make predictions.

python

Copy

```python
import joblib

from flask import Flask, request, jsonify


app = Flask(__name__)


# Load the saved model

model = joblib.load('iris_model.pkl')


@app.route('/predict', methods=['POST'])

def predict():

    data = request.get_json()


    # Extract features from the JSON data
```

225

```python
    features = data['features']

    # Make a prediction using the model
    prediction = model.predict([features])

    # Return the prediction as a JSON response
    return jsonify({'prediction': int(prediction[0])})

if __name__ == '__main__':
    app.run(debug=True)
```

Step 4: Testing the API To test the API, you can send a POST request to the /predict endpoint with the following JSON data:

json

Copy

```json
{
  "features": [5.1, 3.5, 1.4, 0.2]
}
```

The Flask app will use the pre-trained model to make a prediction based on the input features and return the predicted class (0, 1, or 2 corresponding to different Iris species).

Step 5: Deploying the Model API Once the model is integrated into your Flask API, you can deploy the application to any platform, such as **Heroku**, **AWS**, or **Docker**, to allow others to use your machine learning models via API calls.

3. Benefits of Integrating Machine Learning with Flask

- **Easy Integration**: Flask provides a simple and flexible framework for integrating machine learning models into production environments.
- **Real-Time Predictions**: With a Flask API, you can expose machine learning models to make real-time predictions.
- **Scalability**: Flask APIs can be containerized and deployed to cloud platforms that automatically scale based on incoming traffic.

12.5 Advanced API Security: Encryption and Secure Communications

When building APIs, especially those handling sensitive data, security is paramount. **Encryption** and **secure communications** are essential for protecting data in transit and ensuring that unauthorized users cannot access or tamper with your API.

1. Importance of API Security

APIs are often the entry point to sensitive data or systems. If not properly secured, APIs can become a target for various attacks, including **data breaches**, **man-in-the-middle attacks**, and **unauthorized access**. Securing APIs with encryption and secure communication protocols is critical for protecting data and ensuring privacy.

2. Securing Communications with HTTPS

By default, Flask serves content over **HTTP**, which is not secure. To protect your API and ensure secure communication, you should always use **HTTPS** (HyperText Transfer Protocol Secure). HTTPS encrypts the data transmitted between the client and the server, ensuring that sensitive information like passwords, tokens, and personal data are protected.

Step 1: Obtain an SSL/TLS Certificate To enable HTTPS, you need an **SSL/TLS certificate**. You can get a free certificate from **Let's Encrypt** or purchase one from a trusted certificate authority (CA).

Step 2: Configure Flask for HTTPS Once you have the certificate, you can configure Flask to serve content over HTTPS. For local development, you can use **Flask's built-in SSL support** by specifying the certificate and key files.

python

Copy

```
app.run(ssl_context=('cert.pem', 'key.pem'))
```

For production, it's recommended to use a reverse proxy like **Nginx** or **Apache** to handle HTTPS, while Flask serves the API over HTTP.

3. Using API Tokens for Authentication and Authorization

To secure access to your API, you can implement **authentication** and **authorization** using API tokens, such as **JWT** (JSON Web Tokens) or **OAuth**.

JWT Authentication: JWT tokens are commonly used for stateless authentication. They allow users to authenticate once and receive a token that can be used for subsequent requests.

228

- **JWT Generation**:

python

Copy

```python
from flask_jwt_extended import create_access_token


@app.route('/login', methods=['POST'])

def login():

    username = request.json.get('username')

    password = request.json.get('password')


    # Verify user credentials (using a database or hardcoded data)

    if username == 'user' and password == 'password':

        token = create_access_token(identity=username)

        return jsonify(access_token=token), 200

    return jsonify(message='Invalid credentials'), 401
```

- **JWT Authentication Middleware**: To secure an endpoint, use the @jwt_required() decorator to ensure that the user is authenticated before accessing the resource.

python

Copy

```python
from flask_jwt_extended import jwt_required


@app.route('/protected', methods=['GET'])
@jwt_required()
def protected():
    return jsonify(message="This is a protected endpoint")
```

4. Encrypting Sensitive Data

To ensure data confidentiality, sensitive data should be encrypted before being stored or transmitted. Flask can integrate with encryption libraries such as **PyCryptodome** for encrypting sensitive fields like passwords or personal information.

Example: Encrypting Passwords You should never store passwords in plain text. Instead, store **hashed** passwords using a secure hashing algorithm like **bcrypt**.

bash

Copy

```bash
pip install flask-bcrypt
```

python

Copy

```python
from flask_bcrypt import Bcrypt

bcrypt = Bcrypt(app)

@app.route('/register', methods=['POST'])
def register():
    password = request.json.get('password')
    hashed_password = bcrypt.generate_password_hash(password).decode('utf-8')
    # Save the hashed password to the database
    return jsonify(message="User registered successfully"), 201
```

This ensures that even if your database is compromised, the actual passwords remain secure.

5. Rate Limiting and Throttling

To prevent **Denial-of-Service (DoS)** attacks and limit abuse of your API, implement **rate limiting**. Rate limiting ensures that clients can only make a certain number of requests in a given time frame.

Flask-Limiter is a popular extension that can help with this:

bash

Copy

```
pip install Flask-Limiter
```

python

Copy

```
from flask_limiter import Limiter

limiter = Limiter(app, key_func=get_remote_address)


@app.route('/api', methods=['GET'])
@limiter.limit("5 per minute")
def api():
    return jsonify(message="This is a rate-limited endpoint")
```

6. API Security Best Practices

- **Use HTTPS for Secure Communication**: Always serve your API over HTTPS to protect data in transit.
- **Implement Token-based Authentication**: Use **JWT** or **OAuth** for secure, stateless authentication.

232

- **Encrypt Sensitive Data**: Use strong encryption for storing and transmitting sensitive data, such as passwords and API keys.
- **Rate Limiting**: Implement rate limiting to prevent abuse and protect your API from DoS attacks.
- **Regular Security Audits**: Regularly audit your API for security vulnerabilities and apply patches or updates.

12.6 Summary & What's Next

In this chapter, we delved into advanced topics in Flask API development:

- **Machine Learning and Flask**: We learned how to integrate machine learning models into Flask APIs to serve predictions via HTTP requests.
- **Advanced API Security**: We discussed encryption, HTTPS, token-based authentication (JWT), data encryption, and other security best practices to protect your API.
- **API Security Best Practices**: We covered key strategies to ensure your Flask APIs are secure, including authentication, secure communication, rate limiting, and encryption.

In the next chapter, we will explore **API Versioning and Documentation**, where we'll dive into strategies for managing multiple versions of your API and providing clear, developer-friendly documentation.

Chapter 13: Conclusion and Next Steps

13.1 Wrapping Up: Key Takeaways from the Book

As we conclude this journey through Flask API development, it's important to recap some of the key concepts, best practices, and techniques that we've covered. This book has provided you with the knowledge and tools needed to build robust, secure, and scalable APIs using Flask. Below are some of the most important takeaways:

1. Flask Basics and Core Concepts

- **Flask Fundamentals**: We began by covering the basics of Flask—understanding its core components like routes, views, and request handling. Flask's minimalistic approach makes it easy to get started with API development.
- **HTTP Methods**: We covered the main HTTP methods (GET, POST, PUT, DELETE) and how to use them effectively to design RESTful APIs.

2. Building Scalable and Secure APIs

- **Scalability**: We explored strategies for building scalable APIs using techniques such as caching, asynchronous tasks, and load balancing with tools like Kubernetes.
- **API Security**: Security is critical in API development. We discussed how to implement secure authentication (JWT, OAuth), ensure data encryption, and protect APIs from attacks using HTTPS and rate limiting.

3. Advanced Flask API Features

- **GraphQL**: We delved into GraphQL, demonstrating how to build flexible and efficient APIs that allow clients to query data exactly as needed.

- **Machine Learning Integration**: Flask can be used to serve machine learning models, and we covered how to integrate your trained models into Flask APIs to make predictions.
- **Serverless Architectures**: We learned about serverless computing with AWS Lambda and how to deploy Flask APIs in serverless environments for automatic scaling and cost savings.

4. Deployment and Monitoring

- **Deployment**: We covered various deployment strategies, from using platforms like Heroku to Dockerizing Flask apps and deploying them on Kubernetes.
- **Monitoring and Logging**: We discussed how to implement monitoring and logging to track your API's performance, identify issues, and ensure reliability in production environments.

5. Best Practices and Real-World Applications

- **API Design Principles**: Throughout the book, we emphasized the importance of following best practices in API design, such as versioning, pagination, and error handling.
- **Real-World Use Cases**: We walked through examples of building APIs for different use cases, including e-commerce, social media, IoT, and microservices.

By now, you should have a solid understanding of Flask API development, from the basics to advanced concepts, and be equipped with the tools to build, secure, and scale your own Flask APIs.

13.2 How to Continue Learning Flask and API Development

Although you've learned a lot from this book, the world of API development is vast, and there's always more to explore. Here are some ways to continue your learning journey:

1. Build More Projects

One of the best ways to learn is by building real projects. Try creating more complex APIs with Flask by incorporating features such as:

- **User Roles and Permissions**: Implement role-based access control (RBAC) in your Flask APIs.
- **Payment Integration**: Integrate payment systems like **Stripe** or **PayPal** for real-world use cases like e-commerce.
- **WebSocket Integration**: Build real-time applications, such as chat apps or live notifications, using **Flask-SocketIO**.

2. Explore Other Python Web Frameworks

While Flask is a fantastic framework for APIs, there are other frameworks that may suit different use cases:

- **Django**: A full-fledged web framework that comes with many built-in features, such as an ORM and authentication system. Django is a great choice for larger applications.
- **FastAPI**: A modern, fast (high-performance) web framework for building APIs with Python, which uses **Python type hints** to improve performance and developer experience.

3. Contribute to Open Source

Contributing to open-source projects is an excellent way to deepen your knowledge of Flask and API development. Look for Flask-related projects on **GitHub** that need contributions, whether it's fixing bugs, improving documentation, or adding new features.

4. Keep Up with Industry Trends

The tech landscape is always changing, and API development is no exception. To stay up to date:

- Follow blogs and tutorials on **Medium, Dev.to**, or **Real Python**.
- Attend conferences or webinars focused on web development, Flask, and APIs.
- Explore online courses on platforms like **Udemy, Coursera**, or **Pluralsight** for more in-depth learning.

5. Learn About Advanced Topics

If you feel comfortable with Flask, consider diving deeper into advanced topics, such as:

- **Microservices**: Learn how to build distributed systems with Flask and other microservices technologies.
- **API Testing**: Explore advanced testing techniques using tools like **Postman** and **pytest** to ensure that your APIs are robust and reliable.
- **GraphQL**: Deepen your knowledge of **GraphQL** by experimenting with more complex queries and mutations.

6. Study Other API Architectures

While this book has focused on RESTful APIs, there are other API architectures worth exploring:

- **gRPC**: A modern, high-performance RPC (Remote Procedure Call) framework that is ideal for internal service-to-service communication.
- **WebSockets**: Real-time, bidirectional communication between clients and servers, often used for building chat applications, live updates, and gaming.

By continually experimenting, building, and learning from real-world projects, you'll be able to master Flask API development and stay ahead in the field.

API development is a powerful skill that enables you to create dynamic, efficient, and scalable web applications. Flask, with its minimalistic design and flexibility, is an excellent framework for building APIs that cater to a wide range of use cases. Now that you've acquired the knowledge from this book, the next step is to continue building, exploring, and refining your skills.

13.3 Community and Resources for Flask Developers

The Flask community is large, active, and supportive, providing a wealth of resources for developers at all skill levels. Engaging with the community and leveraging the available resources can greatly enhance your learning and development process.

1. Flask Community

- **Flask Mailing List and Forum**: Flask has an official mailing list and a forum where you can ask questions, share knowledge, and engage with other developers. You can join the Flask mailing list through Flask's official website.
- **GitHub**: Flask's source code is open-source and hosted on GitHub. The Flask repository is a great place to contribute, report bugs, or simply explore how the framework works. You can also find many community-driven Flask-related projects on GitHub.
- **Stack Overflow**: Flask has an active presence on Stack Overflow. If you encounter issues while developing with Flask, searching for answers or asking questions with the flask tag is a great way to get help from experienced developers.
- **Reddit**: The **r/flask** subreddit is a community where developers share tips, projects, and troubleshooting solutions related to Flask.
- **Slack and Discord**: There are also various Slack or Discord communities for Flask developers where you can ask questions and interact with other developers in real-time.

2. Flask Documentation

Flask's official documentation is one of the most comprehensive resources available. It includes tutorials, guides, and API references that can help you understand how to use Flask effectively.

- Flask Documentation

3. Tutorials and Blogs

- **Real Python**: A website with a large collection of tutorials for Python developers, including detailed Flask guides.
- **Miguel Grinberg's Blog**: Miguel Grinberg is a well-known Flask expert. His blog and his book "Flask Web Development" provide excellent, in-depth resources for Flask developers.
- **Dev.to**: A developer-focused community with regular posts about Flask, Python, and web development.

4. Online Courses and Books

- **Udemy**: Platforms like Udemy offer comprehensive video courses on Flask development, ranging from beginner to advanced levels.
- **Pluralsight**: Provides professional-level courses and tutorials for Flask and web development.
- **Books**: In addition to "Flask Web Development" by Miguel Grinberg, other great resources include **"Flask By Example"** by Gareth Dwyer and **"Mastering Flask"** by Jack Stouffer.

5. Conferences and Meetups

- **PyCon**: The Python community's major conference, often featuring sessions and talks related to Flask and web development.

- **FlaskConf**: While not as common, you might find dedicated Flask or web development conferences in your area or virtual events.
- **Local Meetups**: Many cities have Python or Flask-focused meetups where you can collaborate with local developers, attend talks, and share knowledge.

13.4 Next Steps: Building Your Own Flask API Projects

Now that you've learned the fundamentals of Flask and how to build APIs, the best way to continue growing as a developer is to build real-world projects. Here are some ideas for projects that will help you hone your skills and develop a deeper understanding of Flask:

1. Create a Personal Blog API

Develop an API that allows users to create, edit, and delete blog posts. Add features like authentication, categories, and comment sections. This will allow you to practice working with databases, implementing CRUD operations, and managing user authentication.

2. E-Commerce API

Build an e-commerce API that includes features like:

- User authentication
- Product management (viewing, adding, and deleting products)
- Cart and order management
- Payment integration (using services like Stripe or PayPal)

3. Task Manager API

Build an API for a task management system that allows users to create, manage, and assign tasks. Add features such as:

- User registration and authentication
- Task prioritization (low, medium, high)
- Due dates and reminders

4. Social Media API

Create a social media API where users can post messages, follow other users, and like posts. Features may include:

- User profiles
- Post creation and interaction
- Friendships and following
- Real-time notifications

5. IoT Data API

Create an API that collects data from IoT devices. These could be temperature sensors, humidity monitors, or other devices, and the API should be able to store data, retrieve it, and possibly trigger actions based on certain conditions (e.g., sending alerts when temperatures exceed a threshold).

6. Machine Learning Prediction API

Integrate machine learning models into a Flask API to serve predictions. This could include:

- Training a model on a dataset (e.g., housing prices or sentiment analysis)
- Exposing the model's predictions via an API endpoint for real-time usage.

7. Personal Finance Tracker

Create an API to track income, expenses, and budgeting for users. Implement features such as:

- Transaction history
- Budget categories (e.g., food, transportation, entertainment)
- Data visualization (e.g., graphs to show spending trends)

8. Integration with External APIs

Develop an API that aggregates data from other services. For instance:

- Weather API: A service that fetches weather data from a third-party API and returns it to users in a structured format.
- News API: Aggregate and filter news articles from multiple sources.

Each of these projects will challenge you to implement new features and explore different areas of API development. As you work on them, make sure to follow best practices for API design, security, testing, and documentation.

13.5 Final Words

Congratulations on completing this book! You now have the foundational knowledge and practical skills to build, secure, and deploy APIs using Flask. By building real-world projects, engaging with the Flask community, and continuing to learn, you can deepen your expertise and take your Flask development skills to the next level.

API development is a dynamic field with continuous advancements, and Flask remains a powerful and versatile framework that can adapt to your needs as a developer. Keep experimenting, building, and staying curious. Your journey in Flask and API development is just beginning, and there are endless possibilities ahead.

Good luck with your Flask projects, and we hope you continue to explore the vast world of API development!

Appendices

A1. Commonly Used Flask Commands and Tips

As you continue working with Flask, you'll likely use several commands and tips to streamline your development process. Here's a list of commonly used Flask commands and development tips to keep in mind:

1. Starting the Flask Development Server

Flask comes with a built-in server for development purposes. Use the following command to start the Flask application:

bash

Copy

```
flask run
```

By default, this runs the application on http://127.0.0.1:5000/.

To run the server on a different port, use:

bash

Copy

```
flask run --port 8080
```

To allow connections from any IP address (useful in a containerized environment), use:

bash

Copy

```
flask run --host=0.0.0.0
```

2. Running Flask with Debug Mode

To enable Flask's debug mode, set the environment variable FLASK_ENV to development:

bash

Copy

```
export FLASK_ENV=development
flask run
```

In debug mode, Flask will reload the server when code changes, and it will display detailed error messages for easy debugging.

3. Running Flask with a Specific Configuration

You can specify different configurations (e.g., development, production) by setting the FLASK_APP and FLASK_ENV environment variables.

bash

Copy

```
export FLASK_APP=myapp.py
export FLASK_ENV=production
flask run
```

This allows you to configure Flask to run in different environments (development, production) with specific settings.

4. Database Initialization

If you're using SQLAlchemy, you often need to create or migrate the database schema. Here's how you can do it using the Flask shell:

244

bash

Copy

```
flask shell
```

Within the shell, you can create or drop the tables like so:

python

Copy

```
from yourapp import db
db.create_all()  # Create all tables
```

5. Running Flask Migrations

To handle database migrations with **Flask-Migrate**, you can use the following commands:

Initialize migrations:

bash

Copy

```
flask db init
```

- Create a migration file:

  bash

  Copy

  ```
  flask db migrate -m "Initial migration"
  ```

- Apply migrations:

  bash

  Copy

  ```
  flask db upgrade
  ```

245

6. Flask Testing

To run tests, you can use the pytest framework. For Flask apps, you can run tests with:

bash

Copy

```
pytest
```

This will automatically discover and run tests from files named test_*.py.

7. Helpful Flask Tips

- **Blueprints**: Break your app into modular components using Flask's **Blueprints** to keep your code organized.

Error Handling: Use Flask's errorhandler decorator to handle common HTTP errors (e.g., 404, 500).

python

Copy

```
@app.errorhandler(404)
def not_found(error):
    return jsonify({'message': 'Not found'}), 404
```

A2. Flask Project Structure Templates

Organizing your Flask application into a clean and maintainable project structure is essential for scalability, especially as your application grows. Below is an example of a well-organized Flask project structure template.

1. Basic Flask Project Structure

bash

Copy

```
/flask_project
  /app
    __init__.py      # Initialize the app and configure extensions
    /models          # Store your data models
    /routes          # Store routes and views
    /templates       # Store HTML templates (if used)
    /static          # Store static files (CSS, JS, images)
  /config.py         # Configuration settings for different environments
  /run.py            # Entry point to run the app
  /requirements.txt  # List of dependencies for the project
  /migrations        # Database migrations folder (if using Flask-Migrate)
```

2. Explanation of the Structure

- **/app**: The main application folder containing the core files.
  - **__init__.py**: Initialize the Flask app, set up configuration, and initialize extensions (e.g., SQLAlchemy, JWT).
  - **/models**: Store all your database models here, usually in separate files for organization.
  - **/routes**: This folder contains your route handlers (views). You can break routes into different modules based on functionality, e.g., auth.py, product.py.
  - **/templates**: Stores HTML templates when using Flask to serve dynamic web pages.
  - **/static**: Contains static assets like CSS, JavaScript, and image files.
- **config.py**: This file stores application configuration, such as environment-specific settings like database URIs, secret keys, and more.

247

- **run.py**: The entry point for running the application. This file will start the Flask app when executed.

requirements.txt: This file contains all the external Python libraries that your app depends on. You can generate it by running:

bash

Copy

```
pip freeze > requirements.txt
```

3. Extended Structure for Larger Projects

If your application grows further, you can extend the structure to include additional folders like:

- **/services**: For services that handle business logic.
- **/utils**: For utility functions that are used across the app.
- **/tests**: Store your test cases and testing setup here.

Example extended structure:

bash

Copy

```
/flask_project
  /app
    /models
    /routes
    /templates
    /static
    /services
    /utils
  /config.py
  /run.py
```

```
/requirements.txt
/tests
    /test_routes.py
    /test_models.py
/migrations
```

A3. Further Reading and Resources

While this book has introduced you to the essentials of Flask and API development, there are many additional resources available to help you continue your learning. Below are some recommended books, websites, and tools for Flask developers:

1. Books

- **Flask Web Development** by Miguel Grinberg: A comprehensive guide that covers everything from basic Flask concepts to advanced techniques like WebSockets and testing.
- **Flask By Example** by Gareth Dwyer: This book covers building real-world applications using Flask, from basic APIs to full-fledged web apps.
- **Mastering Flask Web Development** by Daniel Gaspar: This book explores advanced Flask techniques and best practices for professional developers.

2. Online Resources

- **Flask Documentation**: Official Flask Documentation
- **Real Python**: Real Python Flask Tutorials
- **Flask Mega-Tutorial**: A free and comprehensive tutorial series by Miguel Grinberg. Flask Mega-Tutorial

3. Tools and Libraries

- **Flask-SQLAlchemy**: An extension for Flask that adds support for SQLAlchemy, an ORM for database interaction.
- **Flask-JWT-Extended**: A library to help with handling JWT-based authentication in Flask applications.
- **Flask-Migrate**: Handles database migrations for Flask using Alembic.
- **Postman**: A popular tool for testing APIs, creating and sending HTTP requests.
- **Pytest**: A testing framework for Python that integrates well with Flask.

4. Communities and Forums

- **Stack Overflow**: For asking and answering questions about Flask and API development.
- **Reddit (r/flask)**: A subreddit dedicated to Flask-related discussions.
- **Flask Google Group**: A mailing list for Flask users where you can discuss issues and share insights.

A4. Glossary of API and Flask Terms

To help you better understand the terminology used in this book, here is a glossary of some common API and Flask terms:

1. API (Application Programming Interface): A set of rules that allows one application to interact with another. In the context of web APIs, it refers to the protocols and tools used to request and exchange data between clients and servers.

2. Flask: A micro web framework for Python. Flask is designed to be simple and lightweight, making it easy to build web applications, including APIs.

3. REST (Representational State Transfer): An architectural style for building web services. RESTful APIs are designed around the concepts of statelessness and client-server communication using standard HTTP methods (GET, POST, PUT, DELETE).

4. JWT (JSON Web Token): A compact, URL-safe token format used for securely transmitting information between parties, typically used for authentication.

5. ORM (Object-Relational Mapping): A technique for converting data between incompatible type systems (e.g., between Python objects and relational databases). SQLAlchemy is a popular ORM used with Flask.

6. Endpoint: A specific URL pattern in an API where the client can send a request. For example, /users could be an endpoint for retrieving user data.

7. CRUD: Acronym for Create, Read, Update, Delete. These are the basic operations performed on data in most APIs.

8. Blueprint: A way to organize your Flask application into reusable components, allowing you to break the app into smaller, manageable parts.

9. Middleware: Code that sits between the request and response phases of an API call. Flask supports middleware functions to handle things like authentication and logging.

10. CORS (Cross-Origin Resource Sharing): A security feature that allows or blocks web browsers from making requests to a domain different from the one the page was served from.

11. WebSocket: A protocol that provides full-duplex communication channels over a single TCP connection, allowing real-time data exchange.

These terms and definitions should help you better understand Flask development and API-related topics.